WEIRD FACTS

ABOUT

CANADIAN

HOCKEY

Strange, Wacky & Hilarious Stories

Peter Boer

OVER
TIME
BOOKS

The Publisher: OverTime Books is an imprint of Éditions de la Montagne Verte

Library and Archives Canada Cataloguing in Publication

Boer, Peter, 1977–
    Weird Facts about Canadian Hockey: Strange, Wacky & Hilarious Stories / Peter Boer.

    Includes bibliographical references.
    ISBN-13: 978-0-9737681-2-1
    ISBN-10: 0-9737681-2-6

    1. Hockey—Miscellanea. 2. National Hockey League—Miscellanea. I. Title.

GV847.B53   2005 796.962'64   C2005-904523-X

Project Director: Jay Poulton
Project Editor: Nicholle Carrière
Production: Trina Koscielnuk
Cover Image: Courtesy Getty Images, photo by Bruce Bennett. (Toronto Maple Leafs #13, Mats Sundin; Ottawa Senators #9, Martin Havlat.)

PC: P6

Table of Contents

~•❊•~

Dedication

To Dad and his Bobby Hull–autographed skates:
Great fathers don't need fancy equipment.
Thanks for playing.

Acknowledgements

Like a t-shirt suspended from a parachute, falling from the rafters of the Bell Centre, this book was a gift from stand-up author, photographer and publisher Jay Poulton: thanks for being a great friend. To my mother Faye who, despite 32 hours of labour is still willing to be patient with me, whether in life or in writing: thanks for your support. To my editor Nicholle, for agreeing to tackle another one of my projects: this one won't cost you anything. And lastly, to every coach who ever laced up my skates, gave me a ride home after practice or handed out oranges at intermission: this book—this game—would not be possible without you.

Introduction

In a year that has been best exemplified by the folly of professional hockey, it seems fitting that we pay tribute to the weird, the wacky and the most whimsical moments in the great game's history.

As everyone who follows the game knows quite painfully, the Stanley Cup, a governor-general's tribute to the country and the game he grew to love, was not awarded in 2005. For the first time since the deadly Spanish influenza outbreak that spoiled the Cup matchup between the Montréal Canadiens and the Seattle Metropolitans in 1919, there will be no champion. In all future hockey guides and compendiums, the 2005 season will forever be followed by an asterisk and a footnote explaining that the season was cancelled because of a labour disagreement.

Writing this book was a welcome respite in a season in which the 30 rinks of the National Hockey League sat in darkness. I grew up immersed in the game. I learned to skate shortly after I mastered walking and began chasing the puck around a miniature rink with nine other rinkmates at the age of five. I have played every position on the ice, including a five-year stint as a goaltender that frayed my mother's already jangled nerves. I have refereed and coached. I have minded the score clock, flicked on the goal light, opened and closed penalty boxes, repaired cracks in the ice and scraped up frozen pools of blood.

I have reported on hockey games from both men's and women's leagues, in nearly all levels. The only thing I have yet to do is drive the Zamboni…and it pains me I haven't done that yet.

Researching this book, however, has been a bittersweet task. For as I have sifted through the history of hockey, trying to isolate the game's strangest, most stupefying moments, the futility of the labour strife between the NHL and NHLPA became increasingly poignant.

What stunned me as Gary Bettman and Bob Goodenow, Bill Daley and Ted Saskin, Trevor Linden and Harry Hotchkiss sniped at one another over 10 months, is how quickly hockey fans such as myself adapted to the disappearance of the game. The first few weeks were rough, don't get me wrong—I briefly experimented with a kind of patch to ease the symptoms of withdrawal, but got tired of ripping all my hair out whenever I yanked the tape off my arm. By November, though, I couldn't tell you what had made me so upset. Those of us who traditionally spent Saturday nights glued to CBC Television looked around and, maybe for the first time in decades, saw other ways to occupy our time. We set aside time for our families and friends. We started going out into the world, maybe watching movies or plays or taking in live music. We puttered around the house, fixing creaks and drips, or picked up a book or newspaper. Maybe we introduced ourselves and our children to junior, university or women's hockey.

Many of us who had spent so long watching the game, however, grabbed our skates out of the basement, mashed a tuque topped by a merry puffball over our hair and wandered out into the −20°C winter, looking for a game.

What has brought us to the point where a season without hockey has become little more significant than the latest series of *Survivor*? In my opinion, the reason for the game's current state was best explained by a 12-year-old boy whose first-ever published work, in the January 1990 issue of *Hockey Digest*, began: "I think the idea of expansion in the NHL sucks." Though I can state with relative accuracy that this youngster didn't know at the time exactly why expansion was such a bad idea, his words—okay, *my* words—were prophetic. The NHL has since bloated its lineup to a bottom-heavy 30 teams, adding nine new franchises to the league in 12 years in such dubious locales as Tampa Bay, Columbus, Nashville, Anaheim and—as proof that once bitten does not make twice shy—Atlanta. The effect of this largesse has impacted the league everywhere from the box office to the bench. Adding almost 200 new roster positions to the league effectively watered down the quality of play as third-line grinders quickly became franchise players.

The boredom that has since sunk the game into its current defensive tedium can be directly attributed to expansion. Owners and coaches, needing to attract more fans and revenue with less talent, developed and quickly implemented the dreaded neutral-zone-trap/left-wing-lock/grab-and-hang-on-for-dear-life style of hockey that has snuffed much of the life out of the game. As trapping teams leapt onto the backs of quick-paced offences and slowed them down, the speed of the game, and scoring, began to wane. Any player who could manage 20 goals a season now became a marquee character and demanded a salary to match that status. Teams that could afford it spent money hand over fist, inflating salaries across the board for everyone from a 120-point centre to a fourth-line winger. Players who couldn't get what they felt they were worth where they were, started to look elsewhere, and smaller markets began to suffer. The new expansion teams, unable to raise either their quality of play or the necessary revenue to sign significant talent, quickly slipped into the red, posting millions of dollars in losses. That dip was no more apparent than in January 2004 when the cash-strapped, first-place Ottawa Senators, who had come into the league as part of the expansion, could not honour their players' paycheques.

Although expansion and the subsequent downfall of the game can be blamed on the NHL and, more specifically, Commissioner Gary Bettman, the players share equal, if not more liability for taking advantage of the situation. Those who felt they could get a better deal elsewhere went after it, commanding exorbitant amounts of money for skill sets that, while noteworthy, are far from extraordinary. We all know how much the average salary has ballooned since the continuation of the now-expired collective bargaining agreement. Players maintain their *laissez-faire* approach to the sport, arguing that they should be able to make whatever they want if the owners are willing to pay it. Those owners, however, have little choice. If they don't spend money on the players, they won't make money from fans, advertisers or TV contracts.

I wish every player now commanding $4 million per year in salary could do the same research I did, because I think they would find out something remarkable. The history of our game is made up, first and foremost, of people, of characters, of individuals who could skate, shoot and score a little better than everyone else. It's when you look for the quirks, the oddities, the offbeat stories that the quality—or lack thereof—of those players truly begins to shine. Sometimes the stories described in this book are funny. They make you groan in frustration, wince in imagined pain or shake your head in wonder at how anyone could do anything so stupid. Some stories are so tragic, so heart-wrenchingly unfortunate, they may bring you to tears.

If you had a heart attack while playing a hockey game, would you keep playing? I think there are very few among even the most committed players and fans who would, but that's exactly what Bruce Gamble, a goaltender for the Philadelphia Flyers, did in a 1972 game versus Vancouver. The stalwart netminder suffered a mild coronary event during the first period of what turned out to be a 3–1 win for his team. Gamble didn't realize what had happened until after the game. The 34-year-old goalie never played again, and wisely so.

There would be nothing weird or wacky without the players, of that there can be no argument. Their on-ice heroics are frequently coupled with feats of equal fortitude or dismay, like the legendary King Clancy, who on May 31, 1923, became the only player in the history of the league to play all six positions on the ice in one game. Durable as Clancy may have been, his stamina pales in comparison to the physical toughness of legendary Red Wings–Blues goaltender Terry Sawchuk. The legendary netminder suffered more than 400 stitches throughout his career. There is a rumour that when he took a stick to the eye in a game and had to get three stitches in his eyeball, the masochistic puck-stopper actually had mirrors positioned around his head so he could watch the operation with his good eye. The credibility of this story is enhanced when you consider this is the same goalie who kept the bone chips that he had removed from his elbow every summer in a jar.

As quirky as the players have been, their coaches, managers and owners have risen to the occasion with feats of jaw-dropping insanity. Although Harold Ballard, the tyrannical owner of the Toronto Maple Leafs, fired the late Roger Neilsen in March 1979, he rehired the coaching legend two days later. Ballard wanted the move to be a surprise, so he ordered Neilsen to wear a paper bag over his head until the game started. The classy coach refused, and this could have been the main reason Ballard fired Neilsen again two weeks later.

For as long as there have been players, there have been coaches who have tried to motivate their players to win. Frank Boucher, coach of the 1950–51 New York Rangers, looked as far afield as any coach in the game when his club hit a 12-game losing skid. First, Boucher hired a hypnotist to work with the team. The experiment lasted one game, in which the Rangers suffered a 4–3 loss to the Bruins. Not yet ready to abandon alternative remedies for his team's malaise, one month later the team began using a "magic elixir" made by a local restaurant owner. Although the team's fortunes changed briefly, the Rangers still finished the season in fifth place in the six-team league. Quirky as Boucher might have been, he does not take the cake in this category. Former New Jersey Devils coach Jim Schoenfeld is the only coach on record to trigger a league crisis by suggesting that a referee eat another doughnut.

And while players and their guardians struggle to bring home sports' most storied and vaunted trophy, the league has frequently embarrassed itself in its attempts to keep the game running. Although one could point to the league's most recent labour woes as proof enough, there are still more examples. The NHL decided to prequel the disaster that was the league's expansion in 1994 by hosting an outdoor exhibition game in Las Vegas in 1991 between the Los Angeles Kings and New York Rangers. The 29°C temperature turned the Kings vs. Rangers exhibition tilt into a slushball match, complete with a grasshopper infestation. Fortunately, Kings goalie Kelly Hrudey's helmet-cam recorded the futile exercise in all its glory.

And, of course, where would hockey be without its fans? Those diehard hockey lovers who fork out their salaries for $100 cheap seats and $7 draft beer have done their part in making the game as interesting as possible. Flames fan Tim Hurlburt decided to show his devotion to the Calgary Flames by leaping the glass at the Saddledome clad only in a pair of red socks. Unfortunately, the drunken fan misjudged his leap and fell to the ice, knocking himself out for six minutes. Hurlburt's actions got him on the highlight reels of TV stations across North America, as well as a criminal record.

Funny as many of the stories in this book are, the game has not been without its share of horror. Few who saw it can forget the sight of Buffalo

Sabres goaltender Clint Malarchuk clutching at his throat, trying to stem the ocean of blood spurting from a slashed jugular vein. Although much bally-hoo has been made of Todd Bertuzzi's unprovoked assault on Steven Moore in 2004, the courts intruded long ago on the rinks of professional hockey. Charles Masson of the Ottawa Victorias was acquitted of one count of manslaughter, which had originally been a charge of murder, in the death of Cornwall player Owen McCourt. McCourt died from a blow to the head that officials believed Masson had been responsible for, though testimony at the trial lent enough reasonable doubt to secure Masson's acquittal.

But what is most refreshing of all, in some cases in a humorous fashion and in other ways tragically, is how flawed our hockey heroes can be. It's good to know that even Leafs goaltender Ed Belfour can get so drunk, he tries to bribe a police officer, then vomits on himself. It's also sad to think that former Rangers forward Kevin Stevens can be arrested for smoking crack with a prostitute, while his pregnant wife waits for him at home.

What all these stories prove is that hockey is made up, first and foremost, of people, and people, regardless of their status or their wealth, often act badly. They mess up; they fall down; they do things that boggle the average person's mind. They are as susceptible to happenstance and bad luck as the rest of us schmoes.

They may be superstars, but they are also human.

Now that labour peace has finally come to the NHL, and the puck will drop in October 2006, it is my hope the league and the NHLPA can rebuild the game they very nearly killed.

Hockey is as Canadian as laughing at our southern neighbours, the Americans. Therefore, it seemed only natural to include a few tales of the mishaps and misadventures of the NHL's American players in this book. Brian Berard's tremendous comeback from a serious eye injury that nearly ended his career warrants telling, as does Major Frederic McLaughlin's laughable decision to replace all of the Canadian players on the Blackhawks team with minor league U.S.-born skaters. The Blackhawks dismal finishing record in 1937 is proof that Canadians just make hockey better.

Chapter One

Men Behaving Badly

One fact that often escapes the fans who watch their hockey idols tilt against one another nine months out of the year is that these million-dollar superstars are still, first and foremost, human beings.

Growing up as a young goaltender, I had my share of idols fall from grace. My first idol in memory, Philadelphia Flyers goaltender Pelle Lindbergh, took his team to the Stanley Cup finals against the Edmonton Oilers in the 1984–85 season. He capped off the year by winning the Vezina Trophy. Months later, Lindbergh died in John F. Kennedy Hospital after slamming his Porsche into a retaining wall with double the legal amount of alcohol in his system. Although I found some inspiration in the play of Oilers netminder Grant Fuhr for some years, I was equally disheartened after his suspension for cocaine use in the early 1990s. I gravitated then to Patrick Roy, the winningest goaltender of all time, but again became disenchanted following his now-infamous hissy fit in December 1995 that resulted in his trade to Colorado. Years later, I shook my head again when a locked bedroom door was not strong enough to prevent Roy from continuing an argument with his wife.

We'd like to think our athletes are among humanity's best, with few faults, but not many of us can relate to the pressure that comes from playing before hundreds of thousands of people each year. Some players can rise above that stress, while others look for diversions. Drugs and alcohol are a cancer in our society, and though their use is antithetical in professional sports where bodies must be kept in good working condition, their use still crops up. In a way, every story contained within this chapter is tragic for the personal suffering that must underscore each problem. But other stories can't help but provoke a laugh or two at the thought that these hockey players, these star athletes, are as human as the rest of us.

So let's have a look at some of the players who have made headlines over the years for their off-ice shenanigans.

Spinner Spins Out of Control

From the moment Brian Spencer stepped on the ice, misfortune plagued the young man's career.

The Fort St. James, BC native was drafted by the vaunted Toronto Maple Leafs in 1969. "Spinner" was called up from his farm team in Tulsa to play his first game for the Leafs against Chicago, which was scheduled to be broadcast on *Hockey Night in Canada*. When game time arrived, however, the British Columbia CBC affiliate broadcast instead a Vancouver Canucks–California Golden Seals game. In a bizarre and tragic sequence of events, Roy Spencer, Spinner's father, hopped in his car, rifle in hand, drove to the Prince George CBC station and ordered the staff, at gunpoint, to switch over to the Leafs game. Police officers swarmed the building, and when Roy Spencer exited the building, brandishing his rifle, he was shot dead by three police bullets.

Spinner Spencer tried to make a go of it, even notching a hat trick the weekend after his father's death. He played 10 seasons for Buffalo, the New York Islanders and Pittsburgh, but accumulated only 80 goals, a far cry from what had been anticipated when he was first drafted. Though he tried to fade away into obscurity when he moved to Florida after he retired, he was arrested and charged with capital murder in the death of Michael Dalfo, who had been a patron of Spencer's escort girlfriend Diane Falco. Falco maintained that Dalfo was high on cocaine on the evening of

February 2, 1982, when she had gone to his home and he had abused her. Prosecutors alleged that Spencer had gone to Dalfo's home, driven him away and killed him.

Spencer was acquitted by a jury in 1987, but he never changed his lifestyle. On June 2, 1988, he agreed to drive his friend Greg Cook into Riviera Beach so Cook could score some crack. The pair later stopped at a gas station so Cook could buy cigarettes, where they were accosted by a gun-wielding robber. Though Cook handed over his wallet, Spencer told the robber he had no money. The robber's reaction was loud and deadly—he fired a single bullet that passed through Spencer's arm into his chest, killing him.

It is astonishing that one player with so much potential could fall from grace so quickly.

Big Problems in the Big Apple

In 1976, New York Rangers rookie Don Murdoch made the fans in Brooklyn stand up and take notice.

In just the first half of the 1976 season, the freshman forward racked up 32 goals before being sidelined by injuries. His output was astounding, and Murdoch quickly became the toast of New York. People recognized him everywhere he went. Everyone wanted to be his friend, buying him drinks at local bars and, eventually, exposing him to the world of drug use.

When he returned to play the following season, Murdoch's almost frenetic goal scoring pace dipped considerably. Fans expecting more from the young rookie became disgruntled as they watched Murdoch now flail upon the ice, his goal production markedly lower than the year before. Although many held out hope that Murdoch would be able to turn his play around in time for the next season, the Rangers forward never got the chance. While boarding a plane in New York to return home to Canada during the off-season, an airport security guard found a baggie containing 4.5 grams of cocaine inside his sock.

Murdoch faced punishment on two levels—from the courts as well as from the NHL—and in the end, the courts turned out to be the more lenient of the two authorities. A judge fined Murdoch $400 and handed him a one-year suspended sentence, meaning that he would not have to go to jail. NHL President John Ziegler, however, believed the incident required a stiffer punishment. He suspended Murdoch for the entire 1978 season, but later lifted the suspension after 40 games.

Murdoch never regained the offensive touch that had rocketed him to fame and recognition in New York. He played forgettable stints in both Edmonton and Detroit before fading away into the minors.

Fuhr's Drug Folly

The Oilers of the 1980s were the darlings of the city of Edmonton.

Boasting one of the most star-studded lineups in recent history, the Oilers won four Stanley Cups in five years. Wayne Gretzky was rewriting almost every offensive hockey record in the books, and his supporting cast boasted future Hall of Famers such as Paul Coffey, Mark Messier, Glenn Anderson and Jari Kurri.

The Oilers knew how to celebrate, too. They were seen at local nightspots after most weekend home games. One year, the team even took the Stanley Cup to a local strip club to celebrate their triumph.

In 1986, however, rumours of drug abuse on the team were published in a *Sports Illustrated* article that alleged five players were using illegal drugs. It was later confirmed by the *Edmonton Journal* that Oilers starting goaltender Grant Fuhr, who had grown up in one of Edmonton's satellite communities, was a recovering cocaine addict. The rumours were confirmed by Fuhr's estranged wife, and the NHL acted immediately after the revelations became public. Though Fuhr claimed he had been clean for several years, he spent the first few weeks of the 1990–91 season in a drug treatment facility. On September 27, 1990, the league suspended the 1987 Vezina Trophy winner from play for one year, which was reduced to

60 games by league president John Ziegler. In his first game back with Edmonton following his suspension, Fuhr blanked the New Jersey Devils 4–0.

Fuhr would go on to play another 13 seasons in the league with Toronto, St. Louis, Los Angeles and Calgary before retiring. In October 2003, a soldout crowd at Edmonton's Skyreach Centre gave the netminder a prolonged standing ovation in a pre-game ceremony.

Faux Fax Falls Flat

The increasing sophistication of technology in our society has provided many benefits: faster communication, quicker transactions and easier access to an indescribable amount of information. It has also given those of us who would rather not do the work a fast, quick and easy excuse. Who has not at one time or another blamed their computer or printer for an incomplete assignment? Who hasn't ducked out on a meeting or commitment with the classic excuse: "I didn't get the e-mail."

Claude Lemieux is held in both high and low regard in the NHL. His teammates appreciate his leadership, his puck-handling skills and his feisty style of play. His opponents revile him for his exaggerated swan dives to the ice, his cheap shots and his propensity for writhing about on the ice in pain at the slightest touch. Lemieux's reputation as a faker was consolidated in his years as

a Montréal Canadien when Habs coach Jean Per-
ron refused to allow the team's trainer onto the
ice after Lemieux once again played up an injury
in the hope of getting a penalty.

But in 1995, Lemieux tried to apply his wily
ways to his contract negotiations with the New
Jersey Devils. The team once described by Wayne
Gretzky as a "Mickey Mouse" team in the 1980s
had just eradicated the Detroit Red Wings in four
games straight to bring home the Stanley Cup for
the first time in their history. Lemieux had led the
charge to the finals, bringing all his skill and
unruliness to bear in the lockout-shortened regular season, then winning the Conn Smythe Trophy as the MVP of the playoffs.

That summer, the Devils began negotiating
a new contract with Lemieux in the hope of further prolonging the forward's service with the
club. The team's management offered Lemieux
a three-year, $4.1 million contract. Rather than
dip his toe into the waters of free agency, Lemieux
signed off on the contract, and the Devils assumed
they had their playoff superstar locked in for the
1995–96 season.

Days later, however, Lemieux contacted the
Devils and reneged on the contract. His excuse
was such a product of the 1990s, it is amazing
that it had not before raised its head over any professional sport. Rather than honour the contract
he had agreed to with New Jersey, Lemieux
claimed the contract was invalid because it had

been sent to him by fax. Because his signature was a photocopy rather than an original, the deal could not be represented to be authentic and was therefore null and void.

Angered by their franchise player's attempt to welch on what they believed had been a legitimate deal, the Devils took the matter to the NHL for arbitration. Predictably, the arbitrator ruled in favour of New Jersey and ordered Lemieux to observe the terms of his new contract. No ruling, however, could repair the rift that had grown between the team and its player. Claude Lemieux was promptly traded to the Colorado Avalanche before the season even began, where he would win another Stanley Cup that year.

Time eventually does heal most wounds, especially in hockey. Lemieux returned to the Devils in 2000, where he helped the team win yet another Stanley Cup. After stints with the Phoenix Coyotes and the Dallas Stars, Lemieux has since retired and is now president of the ECHL Phoenix Roadrunners.

Bet You Can't Play Just Once

Pete Rose is the most famous baseball player to not be inducted into the Hall of Fame. In 1989, Rose accepted a lifetime ban from Major League Baseball for betting on professional baseball games, including some played by his own Cincinnati Reds.

Rose is, however, not the only sporting superstar to get himself into trouble by gambling. One of the greatest goal scorers in the NHL also found himself in hot water because of his need to make his sports a little more interesting.

In 2003, *Sports Illustrated* ran a story claiming that former Pittsburgh Penguins scoring sensation Jaromir Jagr, who has since made stops in both Washington to play for the Capitals and New York with the Rangers, had accrued $500,000 in debt to an online gambling site. The site, run by CaribSports out of Belize, leaked the story to *Sports Illustrated* when Jagr stopped making payments to reconcile the debt.

According to CaribSports, Jagr had gotten into trouble betting on professional sports in 1998. The gambling Web page had been configured, however, to make it impossible for Jagr to bet on NHL hockey games. The company eventually came to a resolution with Jagr under which the Czech-born hockey star would repay the site a total of $450,000 on a monthly payment plan. Although Jagr maintained he had repaid the debt by 1999, he also confessed that he had gotten in over his head.

"It was 1998, and I made mistakes. It wasn't smart; it was stupid," Jagr told reporters.

Freedom Costs More Than $1 Billion

Ed Belfour, native son of Carmen, Manitoba, is known as one of the NHL's most reliable goaltenders and fiercest competitors.

The quiet, eagle-eyed netminder has seen his career rejuvenated since he was signed by the Toronto Maple Leafs in 2002, replacing Curtis Joseph in one of hockey's most pressure-packed cities. Since he broke into the league with Chicago as an undrafted college player, Belfour's flop-down style and competitive nature has frustrated both shooters and coaches alike. In 2002, the Vancouver Canucks sent Belfour a bill for repairs—the goaltender had used a hockey stick to trash the Dallas Stars' dressing room after he was pulled from the game. Belfour apparently used the stick with some skill, dissecting two televisions and a VCR, as well as knocking several holes in the dressing room wall.

But Belfour's commitment to victory at any price nearly cost him his reputation as an elite hockey player in March 2000. Dallas police were called to a local hotel after receiving a complaint about a fight between two hotel residents. When an officer arrived on the scene to investigate, he found that Ed Belfour, then the Stars starting goaltender, was the subject of the complaint. The curly-haired hockey player was quite drunk and had been arguing with an unknown female at the hotel. When hotel staff tried to intervene in the disagreement, Belfour started tussling with a 50-year-old employee. Eddie "The Eagle" was no more cooperative with the police. He spat in the direction of the police officers, then kicked at them as they tried to move in to apprehend him. The lawmen had no choice but to Mace Belfour and place him under arrest.

The story, however, did not end there. No sooner had Belfour been placed in the police car, than he began to plead his case to the officers, offering them a cool $100,000 if they'd just forget the whole incident. When the policeman in the car declined the offer, Belfour began increasing the value of the bribe until he finally offered the officer the outrageous sum of $1 billion to let him go. The offer might have seemed more legitimate had Belfour not vomited on himself shortly after he made it.

Rangers Forward Falls Through the Crack

When the New York Rangers flew into Pittsburgh to play the Penguins on January 25, 2000, Kevin Stevens wasn't there.

The Massachusetts-born forward, who had won two Stanley Cups with the Pittsburgh Penguins in 1991 and 1992, and also recorded two 50-goal seasons, was supposed to be in the Rangers lineup for the game, but he was nowhere near the rink.

No, Stevens was in a drug rehab facility, following his arrest two days earlier on a charge of felony drug possession.

Early on the morning of January 23, police officers in St. Louis responded to a complaint of suspicious noises coming from a local motel room. Inside, they found Stevens in the company of a known prostitute, Pamela Velia. Stevens had just finished playing a game against the Blues and was riding around in the back of a cab, smoking crack, when he asked the cabby to pull over and offer Velia a ride. He offered Velia $500 for her company, then the two purchased more crack before checking into a Travelodge. The pair were just beginning to smoke their drugs when police descended on the motel.

At the time of his arrest, Stevens was married with two kids. The morning of his arrest, Stevens' wife was confined to their home because of a complicated pregnancy.

As a first-time offender, Stevens was able to avoid a jail sentence in return for a plea of guilty to a single count of felony drug possession. After his stint in rehab, Stevens played briefly for the Philadelphia Flyers before being traded to the Pittsburgh Penguins, where he played until the end of the 2002 season.

Hockey's Baddest of the Bad Boys

No hockey player of the modern era was as renowned for his fighting ability as Bob Probert.

The 1983 Detroit Red Wings draft pick was the NHL's most notorious enforcer during his years with the league. His reputation as a brawler was so established that squaring off against him was enough for a rookie to establish his own reputation. In September 1995, Oilers draft pick Dennis Bonvie captured the imagination of Edmonton fans when he lined up across from Probert in a pre-season game and muttered the infamous words: "You can make or break my career right now."

But Probert's distinction as hockey's bad boy does not stem only from his on-ice play. The Windsor, Ontario native who had broken into the league with the Detroit Red Wings in 1985–86 was arrested twice in the span of eight months for driving under the influence of alcohol, fined thousands of dollars and had his driver's licence revoked. Probert's problems with alcohol were a foreshadowing of things to come as he continued to deteriorate, graduating from abusing alcohol to cocaine. On March 2, 1989, Probert was arrested by U.S. border guards after a package of cocaine, valued at $1500, fell out of his shorts during a strip search. The response from both the U.S. government and the league was fierce. Probert was banished from the NHL for life, becoming only the fourth player in the league to receive such a suspension. He served a 90-day jail term at a federal penitentiary in Minnesota on a charge of cocaine smuggling, then entered a rehabilitation program. The NHL softened its stance and reinstated Probert on March 2, 1990, under the terms of a work-release program, though he was not allowed to travel with the Red Wings to any games in Canada until 1992.

Although he would later confess that his prison term had been a sobering experience, Probert never seemed to learn his lesson. In July 1994, he was involved in a motorcycle accident in which he sustained serious injuries. Police determined Probert's blood-alcohol level was three times the legal limit at the time of the crash, and that there were also trace amounts of cocaine in his system. The Red Wings washed their hands of their veteran enforcer, claiming the team had never "spent more time on one player and his problems than we have on Bob Probert."

Although he was suspended from the league for the remainder of the lockout-shortened 1994–95 season and ordered into rehab one more time, Probert was signed by the Chicago Blackhawks. In his seven years in Chicago, Probert led the team in penalty minutes in four separate seasons. In 2002, the haunted hockey heavyweight officially announced his retirement from the NHL. His respite from the spotlight, however, would be short-lived. Police in Florida were forced to Taser Probert repeatedly on June 4, 2004, during a street scuffle in Delray Beach. Probert was held without bail on three felony charges, but acquitted by a jury in February 2005.

His life on the edge of the law, however, continued. On July 4, 2005, Probert, now 40, made a court appearance in Windsor, Ontario, on charges of assault and intent to resist arrest. The former NHL enforcer had been taken into custody by the Ontario Provincial Police in the community of Lakeshore three days earlier after the OPP had received a report of a violent man damaging property in the area. When they attended the scene, the man tried to resist their efforts to arrest him.

No trial date has yet been set.

Chapter Two

Radical Hockey Rules

Hockey in the 21st century looks very different from the hockey that was played at the turn of the 1900s. Now that the players and owners have reconciled their differences and can move on with the game, the look of the sport will inevitably change again.

In June 2005, the National Hockey League held a series of research and development games, designed to explore what new rules could best improve the game. Everything was on the table: bigger nets, drastically smaller goaltending equipment, touch-up offsides, no-touch icing, eliminating the red line, moving the blue lines closer to the goal...all were accommodated in three different games watched by some of the teams' general managers.

Many have been critical of the mastodon-like lethargy of the league when it comes to spicing up the on-ice product. Fans have howled for years that lesser-skilled teams were slowing down the game with their neutral-zone traps and left-wing locks, clogging up centre ice and turning what should be a fast-moving game into a slow, plodding tea party. Ideas such as eliminating two-line offsides and implementing no-touch icing have been around for years and gained even more attention during the 2002 Winter Olympics in Salt Lake City, which was a shining example of how good the game can be when players are given room to move. Ultimately, the NHL missed its chance to permanently address most of these issues during the expansion-driven 1990s, when teams both new and old were building new arenas. The NHL could have expanded the size of the ice to the larger Olympic-style sheet, but failed to do so.

Changes, however, are inevitable. Many rules have been altered, corrected or left to melt in the Zamboni scrapings since the NHL first launched play in 1917. A game that originally allowed no forward passing and penalized goaltenders for falling to the ice to make a stop has since evolved, rule by rule, into the game we celebrate today. Many of those changes have been unadulterated successes. Others came on the heels of incidents so bizarre that some corrective action needed to be taken, while other rules were so bothersome, they were scrapped outright.

This chapter details some of the offsides and pitfalls the NHL has experienced since its inception, as it has morphed and hiccupped into its current format.

Fire Threatens Inaugural Season

It was to be expected, in the league's debut season in 1917, that there would be a few growing pains as the newly minted National Hockey League evolved. Although other leagues such as the Eastern Canada Hockey Association (ECHA) and Pacific Coast Hockey Association (PCHA) existed, the NHL was the first truly professional league.

The Montréal Wanderers, one of the original NHL teams, began play in December 1917 with the Montréal Canadiens, Toronto Arenas and the Ottawa Senators. The Wanderers were already one of the winningest franchises in the history of Canadian hockey, having won the Stanley Cup four times in amateur challenge play between 1906 and 1910. Although the Stanley Cup did not yet belong exclusively to the NHL—almost any team in North America could challenge the defending Stanley Cup champion for hockey's Holy Grail—the Wanderers were widely expected to become the NHL's first Stanley Cup victor.

Much was expected of the Wanderers franchise in their inaugural NHL seasons because of their vaunted history. The team started off the season with a talent-stocked team, but a disinterested fan base. In their first game against the Toronto Arenas, the Wanderers scrambled to a 10–9 victory. Despite their strong start, only 700 fans came out to watch the game.

Little did those 700 fans know they would be watching a piece of history: the last Montréal Wanderers game in the history of the National Hockey League. On January 2, 1918, three nights before the Wanderers' next scheduled game against the Toronto Arenas, the Westmount Arena, home of the Wanderers, caught fire and burned to the ground. The franchise owners didn't even try to salvage the team's season—the team had already been hard hit by financial problems because of World War I and was having difficulty recruiting solid players. Rather than look for a new rink, owner Sam Lichenstein folded the team, citing $30,000 in losses.

The NHL, however, was not immediately prepared to accept the Wanderers' resignation from the league. In only its second month of play in its first season, the NHL was now faced with having only three teams in the league, a number that did not lend itself to easy rescheduling or substantial revenues. The NHL would need to take some sort of action to retain their right to sue the owners of the Wanderers franchise for any losses that came from the team's bankruptcy.

So, rather than simply cancel the rest of the Wanderers games and allow the team to drift silently into the annals of history, the league maintained the schedule for another two games. On January 5, 1918, the Toronto Arenas took to the ice at Mutual Arena for a game against nobody. Six players hopped the boards and took the opening faceoff. Seconds into the first period, early NHL superstar Cy Denneny carried the puck the length of the ice and slid it into the gaping goal. The whistle sounded, and the Arenas players left the ice, credited with their single goal and a default victory over a team that hadn't actually played.

A second default victory was given to the Wanderers' next opponents in what would have been the inaugural game in the "Battle of Montréal" against the Canadiens, who have survived as the NHL's oldest and winningest franchise. Following the Canadiens default win, the league finally cancelled the remainder of the Wanderers' schedule. The Toronto Arenas went on to win the league playoffs and play the PCHA Vancouver Millionaires for the Stanley Cup. The five-game series was played in Montréal and switched between "eastern" and "western" rules every game. Western rules permitted some forward passing, as well as a seventh skater or "rover." Vancouver won both games under western rules, but the Arenas came out on top in the remaining three games to become the NHL's first-ever Stanley Cup champions.

Win the Game, Lose the Cup

By the 1930s, the NHL had outlived all of its contemporaries and now possessed sole owner-ship of the Stanley Cup. The league's endurance, however, had come with a great deal of turmoil. By 1934, the NHL had ballooned from three to nine teams, with franchises such as the New York Americans, New York Rangers, Detroit Red Wings, Chicago Blackhawks, Boston Bruins and Mont-réal Maroons joining the league. The Toronto team had undergone two name changes, morph-ing from the Arenas to the St. Patricks, to the now-vaunted Maple Leafs. The Montréal Cana-diens and Ottawa Senators were the only two teams from the first season still playing, but the Senators were in financial peril and doomed to cease operations.

Now that only the teams who played in the NHL competed for the Stanley Cup, the league had adopted a league-wide playoff format to determine the best team of the season. Those two-game playoff series were not only much shorter than today's playoffs, but the winner was also selected differently. What mattered more than winning was total offensive output—the team that scored the most combined goals in a two-game playoff would be declared the winner and would advance.

On two occasions, this bizarre playoff format led to comical finishes. On March 22, 1934, the

Chicago Blackhawks faced off against the Mont-réal Canadiens in the NHL playoffs. The Hawks, who had finished only one point ahead of the Canadiens in regular season play, skated to a hard-fought 3–2 victory over the Habs. Three nights later, the teams met again for the second and final game of the series. When the buzzer sounded at the end of regulation time, the Canadiens were ahead 1–0, but both teams proceeded to play overtime. Why was this necessary? By managing only one goal in the second game, the Canadiens had tied the Blackhawks for total offensive output in the series with three goals apiece. An overtime period was necessary to determine the series winner.

In the end, it was the Blackhawks who found the twine first, winning the series by a margin of four goals to three, even though the final score in the second game was 1–1. Chicago went on to win the Stanley Cup that year.

Two years later, a similar situation emerged, again involving the Chicago Blackhawks, but this time against the New York Americans. The Americans came out flying against the Black-hawks in game one, licking Chicago 3–0 on March 24, 1936. Two nights later, the Hawks fought a hard battle and managed a 5–4 victory over the Americans, but it was not enough. The Americans had scored a total of seven goals in the entire series, two more than the Blackhawks, and were declared the series victor.

Fortunately for all concerned, this playoff format was trashed and a best-of-three series implemented the following year.

Minor Penalty, Major Mistake

Broadcasters have always described it as "the most exciting play in hockey"—the penalty shot. Watching the referee blow his whistle and point dramatically to centre ice always brings the crowd to its feet. Skater versus goalie, staring one another down across the ice, readying themselves for a five-second battle in which victory goes to the player with the fastest mind and most agile reflexes.

The penalty shot has been a part of hockey for years, but, like almost every other staple of the game, it has evolved throughout the game's history. In fact, up until the 1940s, there were two different penalty shots that could be awarded: a minor penalty shot and a major one.

A minor penalty shot involved placing the puck approximately 10 metres out from the opposing team's net and allowing a single skater one shot on goal. No driving to the net, no dekes, just one hard, powerful shot. The major penalty shot was exactly the same as a regular penalty shot is today: a skater takes the puck at centre ice and skates in on goal in a classic breakaway showdown between shooter and stopper.

The minor penalty shot, however, was eliminated from league play in the 1940s after an incident in which Toronto's Jackie Hamilton successfully scored two penalty shot goals in one game—one of each kind, back to back. Boston's Dit Clapper had hauled down Hamilton, and the referee awarded Hamilton a minor penalty shot. The referee, however, suffered what can only be described as a temporary fugue and placed the puck at centre ice. Rather than ask questions, Hamilton snared the puck and dashed in on goal, beating the Bruins goaltender. As the Leafs celebrated, the Bruins howled in protest. Realizing his mistake, the referee placed the puck 10 metres out from the net and allowed Hamilton to take his minor penalty shot. Hamilton blasted it home for another goal.

He was only given credit for the second one.

Organists Beware!

When anyone first hears about this particular league rule, they always ask the same question: Why? Only after it has been explained does the logic behind the ruling become obvious.

Before the invention of cassette tapes, CDs and, more recently, MP3s, a single instrument provided music in hockey—the pipe organ. The organist often sat high above the ice, pounding out rousing, metred songs during breaks in play, encouraging fans to stomp their feet, clap their hands and chant "Let's Go" for their favourite team.

But there is one song, a children's classic, that is forbidden by the league from being played during any game at any time. If you think about it really hard, you can probably guess what it is. Got it yet?

If you guessed "Three Blind Mice," then you know your hockey trivia. That's right, the timeless tune about the terror that three visually impaired rodents inflict on an unsuspecting farmer's wife, who promptly turns around and chops off their tails with a sharp kitchen utensil, is verboten in NHL arenas. If you weren't able to guess the name of the song and are wondering why such a rule exists, consider this: before the league expanded its on-ice officiating crew to two referees and two linesmen at the turn of the 21st century, all NHL games were patrolled by one referee and two linesmen—three officials. Players and fans unhappy with the officiating on any given night are often heard to yell out the phrase, "What are you ref, blind?" Consequently, playing the song "Three Blind Mice" could be seen as a way of provoking anger towards the officiating crew, who are, by league rule, above criticism by players and coaches.

We certainly wouldn't want to hurt their feelings, would we?

Send in the Clowns

Madison Square Garden (MSG) in New York is not the same building it was when it first opened in 1879, but regardless of the moves, the name has never changed.

MSG, however, was not originally designed to host hockey games, even though the New York Rangers have been playing their home games in a building bearing the MSG name since they entered the league. Up until the 1950s, hockey in New York was not the draw that it is today, and subsequently, did not bring in as much money as other events. And one of the more lucrative events the Garden hosted was the circus.

The circus came to town every spring, and its earning power and popularity always superseded that of the New York Rangers. Consequently, up until 1950, the Rangers were never able to host any playoff games on their home ice. Once the circus came to town, the Rangers were out. If they made the playoffs, they had to find some-where else to play.

In 1950, the Rangers plowed through the com-petition in the Stanley Cup playoffs, eventually reaching the final series against the Detroit Red Wings. Even though the hometown Rangers skated at the cusp of hockey supremacy in North America, the circus was not to be interrupted. Rather than play their home games at their home arena, the Rangers took their show across the border, using Maple Leaf Gardens in Toronto as their home rink.

The seven-game series between the Rangers and the Red Wings was a rough one. Detroit took game one 4–1, but the Rangers responded with a 3–1 victory in game two. The teams split games three and four before the Rangers took a 3–2 series lead with a 2–1 victory on April 20.

The Rangers were now one win away from securing a Stanley Cup championship, and the NHL promptly intervened. The league cited an obscure rule that stated that a deciding game in a Stanley Cup final could not be played on neutral ice. The Rangers were scheduled to host Detroit for game six at Maple Leaf Gardens, but now had to find another rink because the Gardens were considered "neutral." The circus was still in town, so the teams couldn't play at MSG.

So the league decided to return the series to the Olympia Arena in Detroit, but the Rangers would be designated as the "home team." The move, however, killed the Rangers' momentum. The Red Wings went on to tie the series with a 5–4 victory in game six, then squeaked out a 4–3 double-overtime victory in game seven to win the Stanley Cup.

Supplanted by the circus from their home ice, the Rangers had effectively become a travelling circus of their own.

What's in a Number?

A player's jersey number can often become as famous as the player himself. After all, who out there doesn't know which player wore number 99, one of the only sweater numbers to be retired league-wide? Which scoring phenom wore the inverted version, number 66? What famous Boston Bruins defenceman's sweater number rhymed with his last name?

For those of you who don't know, the names are Wayne Gretzky, Mario Lemieux and Bobby Orr.

Jersey numbers in the NHL run the gamut from 1 to 98, thanks to Gretzky's retirement. Individual teams have retired many, but there are two kinds of numbers that are not permitted by the NHL to be worn in play. Firstly, nothing over 98 can be used because three numerals will not fit on a traditional hockey jersey.

Secondly, the league now bans any player from wearing the number 00, even though some players in the past sported this number. Flyers great Bernie Parent wore the double zeroes during his one season with the World Hockey Association's Philadelphia Blazers. New York Rangers goalie-turned-broadcaster John Davidson also wore the number during his time in the NHL. The last was Buffalo Sabres goaltender Martin Biron, who wore the double goose egg during a call-up from the minors in 1995–96. The NHL has since banned any player from wearing the number.

In a hundred years' time, when every team has retired every number between 1 and 98, players may have to start wearing fractions and decimals.

Muhammad Ali Knocks Out the NHL

The NHL has rescheduled games in its past for many different reasons: fog, flooding, blackouts, war and falling score clocks. But only once in the league's history has the season's schedule been changed to accommodate another sporting event.

On October 30, 1974, the boxing world was eagerly awaiting one of the most important and highly anticipated fights in boxing history. Former heavyweight champion Muhammad Ali was looking to become only the second fighter to ever regain the heavyweight belt against the current titleholder, George Foreman. The fight, which was scheduled to take place in Kinshasa, the capital city of the Democratic Republic of the Congo (then called Zaire), was dubbed by promoter Don King as "The Rumble in the Jungle."

The fight was scheduled for 5:00 AM in Zaire to accommodate North American viewers. With thousands of fans across the continent eager to watch the heavyweight matchup, the NHL decided to reschedule several games slated for that evening to allow arenas to host live closed-circuit broadcasts of the fight. Games between the Toronto Maple Leafs and St. Louis Blues, as well as the Buffalo Sabres and Washington Capitals, were rescheduled for future dates. The New York Islanders versus the California Golden Seals, along with the Los Angeles Kings and Pittsburgh Penguins matchup were moved back to October 29. Only one game, the Detroit Red Wings versus the Vancouver Canucks, went ahead as scheduled.

Fans who packed arenas in all of the NHL cities didn't much care that their home teams' games had been rescheduled. In the end, Ali stood before Foreman's vicious onslaught, allowing the heavyweight champ to punch himself out before dropping him to the canvas.

Take My Pants...Please!

There wasn't a lot about the 1980s that was particularly attractive or stylish, and that included the NHL.

The bell-bottom pants and glittering chains of the 1970s had given way to plastic jewellery, frizzy perms and soul-less hair-rock. Although hockey teams had managed to maintain a classic look to much of their wardrobe, two teams decided to tinker with their outfits in the 1980s.

Those who can remember it do so painfully, watching members of the Philadelphia Flyers and Hartford Whalers skating up and down the ice in one-piece pants. Rather than stick with the traditional short pants and hockey socks that every other team used, Whalers and Flyers players wore "Cooperalls," ankle-length pants that slipped over a player's protective girdle and kneepads. The menacing black of the Flyers' Cooperalls almost made up for the fashion faux pas, but the garish green glare of the monochrome Whalers' pants and sweaters could not be ignored.

The experiment was brief, lasting only one season in 1982–83, but memorable. At the end of the season, both teams retired their Cooperalls, slipping back into their short pants and socks. As protectors of the league's reputation, the NHL moved to ensure that such fashion crimes were never allowed to happen again, outlawing long pants league-wide.

Fans everywhere breathed a fervent "Thank you."

The Best Player Never to Come Out of Japan

The NHL takes the business of hockey very seriously. As a corporate entity, the league and its administrative officials have never been known for their sense of humour.

This fact was proven in 1974 during the spring amateur draft in which NHL teams selected minor-league prospects for future development. The first round was hit-or-miss as future NHL stars like Clark Gillies, Lee Fogolin and Doug

Risebrough were selected alongside forgettables such as Bill Lochead and Gord MacTavish.

As the secret conference-call draft stretched into the 11th round, Buffalo Sabres general manager Punch Imlach, fed up with the tedious, time-consuming process, decided to have a little fun at the league's expense. When the time came for Buffalo's 11th pick, 183rd overall, Imlach announced the Sabres were selecting a Japanese hockey player, Taro Tsujimoto, who apparently played for the Tokyo Katanas of the Japanese League.

No one in the NHL had ever heard of Taro Tsujimoto, so no one bothered to question the Sabres' choice. The pick was allowed to stand and later reported by the media, including the *Hockey News*, as a legitimate selection. Weeks after the draft, Imlach finally admitted to the media and the NHL that Taro Tsujimoto did not actually exist. The Japanese superstar was a creation of Imlach's bored imagination, based on a name he had found in a Buffalo-area phone book. The Tokyo Katanas translated roughly into English as the Tokyo Sabres.

NHL president Clarence Campbell, however, did not see the humour in the joke. For recording purposes, Buffalo's 183rd selection was entered as an "invalid claim," and the team was prohibited from making a replacement pick. The admission, however, came after several NHL media guides had been published for the upcoming season citing Tsujimoto as a Sabres prospect.

Although he never played a game of hockey, Taro Tsujimoto is, to this day, cited in Buffalo's official team media guide.

Would You Like Fries With That?

Nowadays, it isn't unusual for a goaltender to keep a bottle of water on top of his net and sip at it during stoppages in play. This staple of the game, however, is barely 20 years old.

In 1984–85, Philadelphia Flyers goaltender Pelle Lindbergh was the toast of the NHL. The Swedish-born puck-stopper had erupted into the league two years previously, turning in a stellar regular season that would see him awarded the Vezina Trophy as the year's best goaltender. Lindbergh and backup goalie Bob Froese led the Flyers through a highly charged Stanley Cup run that season, which pitted the Flyers against the high-scoring, defending champion Edmonton Oilers.

Lindbergh was also the very first goaltender to keep a water bottle on the mesh of his net. The lanky Swede dehydrated quickly and found sipping at a water bottle helped keep him sharp. The Oilers, however, could not accept this new idea and used the media to publicly humiliate Lindbergh. Edmonton coach Glen Sather commented that Lindbergh shouldn't be setting up a "lunch buffet" in the net. Future Hall of Fame winger Glenn Anderson chimed in as well, asking reporters: "What are they going to want up there next, a bucket of fried chicken?"

The NHL agreed with the Oilers and ordered the bottles removed from the nets. Lindbergh's play in the Stanley Cup finals consequently tumbled as his body fought the impairing effects of dehydration.

It was not the first time Lindbergh's play suffered because of psychological torment. In his rookie season, the young Swede's confidence was shattered when his teammates allegedly subjected him to the crass and humiliating rookie initiation known as "the Shave." As several teammates held the writhing goaltender to the ground, the rest of the team reportedly took turns shaving off all the Swede's pubic hair.

Lindbergh's play plummeted in the Stanley Cup final, and he was pulled from the nets for the last game of the series in favour of Froese. The Oilers shelled Froese in game five, beating the Flyers 8–3 to win their second Cup in two years.

Though Lindbergh would go on to win the Vezina Trophy as the league's best goaltender, his career would not see another spring. Lindbergh died on a New Jersey freeway on November 12, 1985, after drunkenly piling his Porsche into a retaining wall.

Every goaltender now keeps a bottle of water handy during games and practices. It's a shame

Lindbergh did not have time to leave a more enduring legacy.

Playing Hockey in a Heat Wave

Looking back, September 27, 1991, is a date the NHL would just as soon forget.

At the time, the league was eagerly trying to expose the game of hockey to as many new markets as possible in a bid to shore up expansion teams. Franchises were coming on stream in San Jose, Tampa Bay and Miami, geographic locations in which a half inch of snow can paralyze an entire city for a week.

In its haste to publicize the game south of the border, the NHL took a risk in scheduling an exhibition game in a city where the only gaming of note takes place inside casinos: Las Vegas, Nevada. Not only would the Los Angeles Kings and New York Rangers play a game in a city where the temperature seldom slips below 25°C, the game would be an outdoor evening affair. Although an NHL-sized rink was built outdoors at Caesar's Palace, no dressing rooms were available for the players—they were forced to walk through the hotel's casino before and after the game.

The temperature that night was a crisp, cool 29°C, a perfect night for an outdoor hockey game. As the sun set over the Nevada desert, high-powered floodlights swept the expanse of the ice, lighting up the exhibition game. Much to the organizers' shock and dismay, ice conditions deteriorated horribly as the puck became bogged down in piles of slush and water. In addition, the outdoor lights had an unexpected side effect as hundreds of grasshoppers swarmed onto the rink, drawn to the ice by the high-wattage beams. Kings goaltender Kelly Hrudey became the first goaltender in the NHL to wear a helmet-mounted camera during the game, capturing the ice-level action for all to see.

It's probably safe to say the league has no interest in reviewing the footage.

A Toe Too Far

"The Stanley Cup Winning Goal That Never Was" will go down in history as one of the NHL's most embarrassing moments.

The Buffalo Sabres were competing against the high-powered Dallas Stars in the 1999 Stanley Cup finals. The Stars, the regular season points leaders, were leading the series 3–2 with game six scheduled to take place in Buffalo on June 19.

It had been a trying year for players and fans alike. The NHL was clamping down hard on crease infractions. Video goal judges enjoyed sweeping powers, able to disallow a goal if so much as an opposing player's toenail crossed the goal line before a goal was scored. Replays had

overturned hundreds of goals during the regular
season and dozens more during the playoffs. And
the whole issue was ready to cast an embarrassing
pall over the Stanley Cup finals.

The Stars and Sabres battled to a 1–1 tie at the
end of regulation play in game six and proceeded
to play two overtime periods. The stakes were
high—a Buffalo goal would send the series back
to Dallas for a seventh and deciding game,
whereas a Dallas goal would clinch the Cup.

At 14:51 of the third overtime period, 22 seconds shy of becoming the longest game ever
played in the Stanley Cup finals, the unthinkable
happened. Stars sniper Brett Hull drove towards
Sabres goaltender Dominik Hasek and fired a shot
on goal. Hasek made the first stop but gave up a
generous rebound that Hull kicked up to his stick.
As Hull brought the puck forward, his left skate
inched into the crease before the puck. Hasek
couldn't recover to make the stop, and Hull
banged home the Stanley Cup–winning goal.

As soon as the goal judge's light flared, fans and
media began to stream onto the ice, barraging the
players with the flash of strobe lights and inane
questions about how it felt to win the Cup. Buffalo's protest, that the goal had been illegal, fell on
deaf ears.

Though the replay clearly shows Hull's skate in
the crease before he shoots the puck, the NHL
spent the next few weeks justifying the goal.
Rather than admit there had been a serious

mistake, the league explained that Hull had not lost possession of the puck when Hasek had stopped him on the first shot. Therefore, because he was still in possession of the puck, Hull was allowed to be in the crease.

The NHL's confidence in the crease rule, however, did not survive the summer. No sooner had the league tried to defend the indefensible than they scrapped the rule altogether, softening it up to ensure that players weren't interfering with the goaltenders while allowing some leeway with crease infractions. The change, however, came too late for the Buffalo Sabres and their fans.

Coach Lindsay Ruff's public proclamation of "no goal" was the most accurate assessment to come out of the entire ordeal.

Chapter Three

Crazy Coaches

It is a timeless axiom in any sport: when the team is playing poorly, you can't fire the team, so the coach has got to go.

A coach in professional hockey truly occupies one of the most pressure-packed positions in the entire game. The success or failure of his team determines his future. Success is evaluated in wins and Stanley Cups, while failures are public losses for all to see and read or hear about. As soon as a team begins to stumble, the media instantly begin to ponder the security of a coach's job. As soon as those pontifications begin, the axe inevitably falls.

Getting fired in the NHL, however, means absolutely nothing when it comes to future employment. There are few coaches—ex-Sabres coach Ted Nolan being the most poignant exception to the rule—who are not eventually given another opportunity by a different team, if not the same team. Pat Burns, Mike Keenan, Marc Crawford and the now-departed Roger Neilsen are examples of coaches who have rebounded from a job loss—in some cases, three or four—to appear behind the bench of another team.

So why do so many coaches end up being fired every year? Ultimately, the responsibility falls to the team. If a coach and his team can mesh, gel and understand one another's expectations, success on some level is inevitable. If players refuse to "buy into" a coach's system, such as the ennui the Dallas Stars developed that led to Ken Hitchcock's release from the team, the coach doesn't stand a chance.

That's not to say there have not been coaches with ideas that were just fundamentally bad. There are those who simply cannot handle the limelight or pressure of the NHL. There are also those who have tried to be revolutionary in their strategies and training, only to be rebuffed by the players and management. And there are coaches who have simply been unable to win over their teams. As soon as the team tunes a coach out, he might as well start dusting off his résumé because nothing will bring the players back.

The responsibility for assembling the team falls to the general manager, who wheels and deals talent like a used-car salesmen, trying to find the winning formula. Building a team has little to do with whipping out your chequebook, as New

York Rangers general manager Glen Sather is finding out. Despite an $80 million payroll that has listed names such as Jaromir Jagr, Eric Lindros, Brian Leetch and Mark Messier, the Rangers haven't made the playoffs since Sather, or "Slats" as he is known, left the small market of Edmonton behind.

Some men crack, some men crumble. Some establish a glowing legacy that shines through the annals of hockey history, while some fade to little more than a footnote in a book. This chapter is dedicated to the men who stand behind the bench and the men who stand behind them, axe in hand, waiting to swing.

Patrick Goes Above and Beyond

Those who can, do. Those who can't, teach.

It's a common refrain, most often reserved for school teachers and sports coaches. Many coaches, however, especially in the NHL's history, have been able to both do and teach, sometimes in the span of one game.

In April 1928, the Montréal Maroons faced off against the New York Rangers in the Stanley Cup finals to determine who was the best in the 11-year-old NHL. It was another year in which the Rangers were forced to play for the Stanley Cup away from Madison Square Garden, supplanted again by the circus. The entire season was played in Montréal on the Maroons' home ice.

The Maroons came out strong in game one, blanking the Rangers 2–0. In game two, the Rangers had fought to a 1–0 lead when their goaltender, Lorne Chabot, fell to the ice, blood streaming from a cut above his left eye. With their only goaltender forced off the ice for repair, the Rangers were desperate to find a replacement. At first, they tracked down Alex Connell, an Ottawa Senators goalie who had gone six games earlier in the season without allowing a goal, who was seated in the audience that night. The Maroons, however, protested and wouldn't allow Connell to dress. With no one else available to tend the goal, 44-year-old Rangers coach Lester B. Patrick suited up and skated out to replace Chabot.

It should have been a shooting gallery for the Maroons, but the Rangers clamped down defensively in front of their coach and checked hard. Of the shots the Maroons did manage to squeak in on goal, 19 in total, Patrick successfully turned aside all but one. With the score tied 1–1, the game went into overtime, and the Rangers potted the winner.

Rather than pursue his newfound talent, Patrick willingly yielded the twine to Chabot, who returned for the rest of the series. Although the Maroons would blank the Rangers a second time in game three, New York rallied for 1–0 and

2–1 victories in the next two games to win the Stanley Cup.

The Rangers Cup win made huge headlines in New York, but Patrick's spontaneous goaltending debut was hailed as the real story in the victory.

Smythe Gambles on Clancy...Literally

Few general managers today would be willing to put their own money on the table to build the team they want.

In 1930, however, Toronto Maple Leafs general manager Conn Smythe found himself in a dilemma. The Ottawa Senators, once the most dominant team in the entire league, were struggling just to make ends meet. Their financial situation had been deteriorating for years, and as the 1930 season approached, the team decided to take drastic action. In what would ultimately prove to be little more than a band-aid solution for a team that was hemorrhaging fiscally, the team decided to sell its best player for $35,000 to the first team that came up with the funds. That player was Frank "King" Clancy, the Senators marquee defenceman who had notched up 17 goals and 23 assists in 44 games the previous year.

The Leafs' board members, however, were less than impressed with the Senators' asking price. Although Smythe pushed the board hard to come up with the cash to acquire a player who would become an instant fan draw, the board declined, offering only $25,000. If Smythe wanted Clancy badly enough, he was going to have to come up with the other $10,000 himself.

The board probably expected that Smythe would let the matter drop, and most general managers, especially today, likely would have. Smythe, however, was so convinced of Clancy's skill, he refused to give up. One day, the Leafs GM headed down to the racetrack, where he had several horses racing. Smythe reached into his pocket and plunked down $200 on Rare Jewel, one of his own horses, which had yet to win a single race. On this particular day, Rare Jewel was a 106-to-1 longshot to win.

And she won.

Smythe happily returned to work the next day, having grown his $200 bet into an $11,000 win in a single race. Smythe presented the board with $10,000 and promptly bought Clancy's rights, bringing the diminutive defenceman to the Leafs. The Irishman was an instant draw as hockey fans packed the newly built Maple Leaf Gardens in the 1930s to watch the talented defenceman. Clancy would remain a Leaf until he retired in 1936, then would later coach the team for two seasons in the 1950s.

Both Conn Smythe and Frank "King" Clancy have since been inducted into the Hockey Hall of Fame. Both have trophies that are awarded annually in their honour.

The Blackhawks' Bench Blues

For coaching drama and front-office turmoil in the 1930s, no hockey fan needed to look further than the Chicago Blackhawks.

The team's owner, Major Frederic McLaughlin, was an eccentric hockey boss, intent on inserting himself into the team's daily affairs, hand-picking coaches and, from time to time, even the players on his team.

In 1932, McLaughlin met a young Canadian coach named Godfrey Matheson on a train. Matheson's most notable accomplishment to that date had been leading a Winnipeg midget team to a league championship. After the train ride, McLaughlin offered Matheson the head coaching position for the Chicago Blackhawks.

Matheson had a unique style of coaching that McLaughlin found fascinating and believed would revolutionize how the game of hockey was played. Instead of leaving the on-ice play up to the players, Matheson believed in exercising as much control as possible over his team. To do so, Matheson had created a "whistle system" of dictating play. While the players skated around on the ice during a game, Matheson would direct the play from the bench by blowing a whistle. One blast on the whistle was a cue for the player with the puck to pass. Upon hearing two toots, the player was supposed to shoot. Three shrill blasts on the whistle were a cue for the entire team to start concentrating on defence.

The idea seemed sound on paper, but the entire system fell apart on the ice. Players making split-second decisions in the fast-moving game often became confused, forgetting how many whistle blasts stood for which action. They passed when they should have shot and vice versa. Sometimes they didn't hear the whistle at all. Many of the players simply didn't buy into Matheson's system, ignoring the man's frantic whistling altogether.

The experiment lasted all of two games, both of which Chicago lost. Matheson was subsequently turfed by McLaughlin and replaced by Tommy Gorman. Gorman was a more traditional hockey coach with a fiery temper and competitive spirit. Gorman, too, would make hockey history, becoming the first ever hockey coach to be fined by the NHL.

In March 1933, the Blackhawks were playing against the Boston Bruins when Bruins forward Marty Barry bulged the twine in overtime to give his team a 3–2 lead (in the early days, overtime was not sudden death). Gorman instantly became livid, protesting the goal as vociferously as he could. When referee Bill Stewart skated by the Blackhawks bench, Gorman reached out and grabbed the official, shaking him and pulling his sweater over his head. Stewart turned around, and the two began to trade punches at the Chicago bench. When the linesmen intervened, Stewart ordered Gorman off the ice, but the

Chicago coach refused to budge. Several members of the Boston Police Department eventually escorted Gorman from the bench to the dressing room, followed by the entire Blackhawks team. Despite Stewart's warnings, the players refused to return to the ice. After counting down one minute, Stewart promptly awarded the victory to the Bruins, and Gorman was subsequently fined $1000 by the league.

Gorman would not be the last coach ever fined for assaulting a referee during a game. In fact, Jack Adams, coach of the Detroit Red Wings in 1941, in whose honour an annual award is given to the league's best coach, was suspended by the league during the 1941 Stanley Cup finals for rushing referee Mel Harwood. The Red Wings, who were leading the Toronto Maple Leafs 3–1 in the best-of-seven finals, imploded without their coach, losing the next three consecutive games and the Cup.

The bad blood between the Blackhawks and Bill Stewart eventually settled. Five years later, Stewart was re-hired as the Blackhawks' coach and piloted the team to a Stanley Cup championship.

That championship was preceded, however, by another McLaughlin experiment that backfired. The 1937 Blackhawks were destined for last place in the league with five games left in the season. McLaughlin decided the team's fundamental flaw stemmed from the nationalities of its players. The owner declared his team would field only American players for the rest of the year, and McLaughlin backed up his claim by offering contracts to half a dozen minor league players of American lineage. McLaughlin's patriotism, however, could not cover up the fact his U.S.-born-and-bred lineup lacked talent. Of their five remaining games, the Blackhawks lost four, three of them by four goals or more.

Only in New York...

The 1950 New York Rangers were willing to try anything to win, no matter how far-fetched or bizarre the idea was. Of the two new tactics they brought to the dressing room in 1950, neither worked. The team was mired in a 12-game losing streak with the season winding down, and nothing seemed to be working to pry the team out of its extended funk.

Rather than shuffle the lines or the roster, coach Frank Boucher decided to try a more unique approach to help the team overcome its losing ways. Before a game against the Boston Bruins, Boucher hired a hypnotist, Dr. David Tracy, to work with the team before the players took the ice. Tracy tried to use hypnosis to encourage the subconscious minds of the Rangers to reach past their so-so play and truly work hard for success.

The freshly inspired team took to the ice, ready to unleash their newfound psychological power on the Bruins. When the final buzzer sounded, the Bruins had won 4–3, extending the blue-shirts' losing streak to a 13th game. Boucher chose not to invite Dr. Tracy back for another hypnotherapy session with his players.

Rather than shrug off their experimentation with the out-of-the-ordinary in attempting to snap the losing streak, the Rangers decided to knock back their hypnotherapy with a magic chaser. After another month passed without any changes in the team's fortunes, the players began swilling a "magic elixir" to bolster their strength. The potent potion was the creation of New York restaurateur Gene Leone. Although its contents are not known, the strange brew had an intoxicating effect on the Rangers lineup, if only for a short period of time. The team finally began to win as the season wound down, losing only two of their next 13 games. When word of their new secret dietary weapon hit the news, Leone's magic elixir became very popular throughout the entire city of New York. The team's success, how-ever, was short-lived. The Rangers eventually chugged into spring in fifth place in the six-team league with an unimpressive 20–29–21 record, missing the playoffs.

Shore Goes off the Deep End

As a player, Eddie Shore became one of hockey's greatest and toughest defencemen, punishing opposing players with his explosive body checks and flailing fists. As an owner, Shore derailed as many careers as he had as a player and caused just as much pain and discomfort.

After retiring from play in 1947 as a blueliner with the Springfield Olympics of the American Hockey League (AHL), Shore scrounged up enough cash to buy the team outright in 1950. The Stanley Cup winner, however, took a less established approach to improving his team's skills and overall health. Shore insisted all of his players study ballet and tap dance, making them practise in hotel lobbies during away games, as well as on the ice. He would tape his goalies to the crossbar of the net while the rest of the team fired on the helpless puck-stoppers in an effort to teach his netminders to stand up straighter.

When the situation required it, Shore was never afraid to shake up the roster. He once traded future Los Angeles Kings general manager Jake Milford for two hockey nets, then was later overheard complaining about the quality of the nets he received in the deal.

Whenever a player suffered an injury, Shore subjected the unlucky soul to his own rigorous treatments. The Bruins great told anyone who would listen that he had not only survived more than half a dozen heart attacks, he had also cured himself of cancer. Although he had no medical or chiropractic training, Shore would crack the bones and joints of any Springfield player suffering from a physical ailment. One of those players was CBC *Coach's Corner* host Don Cherry.

"Some players were terrified to get on that medical table," said Cherry.

Shore also tried to look out for the psychological well-being of his players. One day, all of the players' wives were invited to the rink for a get-together. Rather than allowing his guests to sip tea and eat tiny sandwiches, Shore lectured the ladies for close to an hour on the perils of sex. His team, he told them, was suffering because their home lives had become too affectionate, sapping the strength of the players. Shore wrapped up the lecture by pleading with ladies to abstain from any "recreational activities" until after the Olympics' playoff run was over.

There is no word on whether or not Shore obeyed this particular edict himself during that playoff year. He was too busy parking cars before every Olympics home game to have much time for any sort of social life.

Uproar in Québec

The residents of the province of Québec have always been protective of their language and heritage. In fact, an NHL coach once infuriated the entire province with an unpopular dressing-room language policy that would lead to the trade of one of the province's most successful goaltending products.

No one on the Philadelphia Flyers seemed to like Vic Stasiuk very much, but the four French Canadian players on the team had more reason to dislike their coach than the rest of the team. Future goaltending great Bernie Parent, who had been raised in Québec, along with fellow French Canadians Jean-Guy Gendron, Simon Nolet and Serge Bernier, were all players on the Flyers' roster who became dissatisfied with Stasiuk's coaching abilities. Their reason, however, was more personal. During the 1970 season, Stasiuk had issued a coach's edict forbidding any of the players from speaking French in the locker room. English was the only language that would be permitted.

After stewing about Stasiuk's language policy, the Québec-born players decided to take action. Parent decided to take the matter straight to the press and leaked Stasiuk's controversial stance to the media. The response in Québec was fierce. The entire province howled in collective outrage at what was seen as a racist policy that undermined the contributions the people of Québec had made to the NHL throughout the league's history.

The league was also not impressed with Stasiuk's stance on speaking French in the Flyers' dressing room. The coach was hauled before a hearing with NHL president Clarence Campbell, during which Stasiuk denied ever making any such declaration. While he protested his innocence, Stasiuk singled out the one player who had caused the entire ruckus. Stasiuk talked with the Flyers' management and arranged to trade media rat and future goaltending great Bernie Parent to the Toronto Maple Leafs.

The rest of the team never really got on board with Stasiuk, who was described by Flyers player Joe Watson as "…an interesting guy. Not a real good coach, but an interesting guy."

At the end of the 1970–71 season, the Flyers management fired Stasiuk, who would go on to coach the Oakland Golden Seals and Vancouver Canucks before retiring in 1973.

Once Stasiuk was gone, the Flyers traded with the Leafs to reacquire Parent's services as a goaltender. It's a good thing they did. Parent would lead the "Broad Street Bullies" to two Stanley Cup championships during the 1970s.

The Point of Victory

Red Kelly has been both a star player and a coach to the Toronto Maple Leafs during his time in the league. He even served as a member of Parliament while he was still a player.

In 1976, Kelly was behind the bench for the Leafs as the team's coach, trying to rally his star, Darryl Sittler, and the rest of the Leafs to a Stanley Cup victory. Kelly's approach to motivating his players, however, was unique. Shortly before the playoffs began, Kelly had come across a magazine article detailing the mystic and cosmic powers of the great pyramids of Egypt. The article left an enduring impression on the coach, who decided to try and muster that paranormal energy to help the team in its upcoming Stanley Cup run.

A large pyramid was assembled and hung from the ceiling of the Toronto Maple Leafs' dressing room in an effort to harness whatever mystical powers the pyramid might be able to impart to the team. Kelly took his new obsession one step further, placing smaller pyramids beneath the players' bench. The theory was that sitting directly on top of the pyramids would enable players to tap into a cosmic force that would make them perform better out on the ice.

Sittler decided to give it a shot first, and the results were remarkable. The Leafs forward promptly scored five goals, resulting in an 8–3 drubbing of the Philadelphia Flyers in the 1976 playoffs. The rest of the team instantly embraced the idea, jockeying with one another for seats on the players' bench closest to one of the pyramids whenever they weren't out on the ice. The power of the pyramids, however, was not absolute, as the Leafs eventually fell to the Flyers in seven games. The pyramids disappeared from Maple Leaf Gardens.

Meet Roger Neilsen's Replacement...Roger Neilsen!

Harold Ballard always had to do things differently. He was legendary for stunts such as printing the names of his players on the backs of their sweaters in letters so small that no one could read them, and his eccentricities go hand in hand with the storied history of the Toronto Maple Leafs.

So when Ballard fired Roger Neilsen in March 1979, just a few weeks shy of the end of the season, everyone had a feeling that the sneaky old coot was up to something. For days, the media in Toronto were atwitter with speculation about who the next Leafs coach would be. Ballard chose to keep the identity of the new coach a secret, right up until the opening faceoff of the team's next game.

No one, however, could have predicted what Ballard would do next. Two days after firing Neilsen, who is remembered in history for his

ugly ties and his pioneering use of video to cri-
tique his own team's performance, Ballard had a
change of heart and decided to hire Neilsen back
to finish the rest of the regular season. Ballard
told Neilsen that he wanted the matter kept quiet
until the team's next game. In fact, Ballard told
the coach, he wanted Neilsen to wear a paper bag
over his head until the opening faceoff. Neilsen,
however, refused to give in to Ballard's ridiculous
demand and emerged from the Leaf's dressing
room that night to a standing ovation from the
fans at Maple Leaf Gardens.

The bittersweet relationship between Ballard
and Neilsen, however, was short-lived. When the
season ended, Ballard refused to offer Neilsen
a new contract.

One thing is for sure—even if Nielsen had
worn the bag over his head as Ballard demanded,
whatever hideous tie he had selected for his
ensemble that day would have likely given away
his identity.

"Mmmmm...Doughnut!"

Never before has so much calamity ensued
because of a single deep-fried pastry.

The New Jersey Devils were the darlings of the
league in the spring of 1988. The team, once
described as a "Mickey Mouse organization" by
Wayne Gretzky, had finally picked themselves up
out of the basement of the NHL and had actually

made the playoffs, owing in part to rookie goal-tender Sean Burke's sensational play.

After cruising through the first two rounds, the Devils soon found themselves in unfamiliar waters, playing against the Boston Bruins for the Wales Conference championship. The winner would go on to face the three-time Stanley Cup champion Edmonton Oilers in the finals.

Game three, however, did not go as the Devils had hoped. After the game, Devils coach Jim Schoenfeld, seething with rage over the officiating of referee Don Koharski, sought Koharski out. When he finally tracked down the portly referee, Schoenfeld exploded, yelling at the official about his poor work and berating him for several missed calls and unnecessary infractions. He bumped up against Koharski, knocking the referee to the ground in front of a crowd of media and onlookers. As Schoenfeld was pulled away from the prone referee, he got in one final verbal shot.

"Have another doughnut, you fat pig!" the irate coach screamed at Koharski.

Upon hearing of the incident, the league briefly reviewed what had happened and decided to suspend Schoenfeld for the rest of the playoffs.

That should have been the end of it, but the Devils were not willing to throw away their successful post-season, of which Schoenfeld had been an important part, so quickly. The team went to court in the U.S. and successfully obtained a restraining order against the NHL. This meant that, legally, the league's suspension of Schoenfeld was itself suspended, meaning that Schoenfeld could coach his team in game four. When the Devils met the Bruins for the next game of the series, Schoenfeld was behind the bench. That fact infuriated referee Dave Newell and linesmen Ray Scapinello and Gord Broesker. Just before the game was scheduled to start, officials got word that neither the referee nor the two linesmen would officiate the game, in protest of Schoenfeld's presence on the Devils' bench.

Game and league officials instantly went into panic mode, scrambling to find a replacement crew to work the game. They turned to the fans in the stands and eventually were able to convince amateur linesmen Vin Godleski, 51, and Jim Sullivan, 50, along with amateur referee Paul McInnis, 52, to officiate. These three men, who had come to the game thinking they were going to be spectators, were now responsible for officiating it. With no officiating jerseys available, the trio took to the ice after a major delay, wearing yellow practice jerseys, green pants and borrowed skates.

The Devils used the situation to their advantage, winning game four of the series 3–1. Schoenfeld eventually relented and served his suspension in game five. The legal victory was really the only one for the Devils in the series, as Boston would go on to win the series, but eventually lose to the Oilers in the Stanley Cup finals.

Thanks for All the Help... You're Fired!

If you look closely at the Stanley Cup, on the band depicting the winning team of the 2000 finals, you'll see Robbie Ftorek's name.

The former Devils coach, however, was not behind the bench when the Devils defeated the Dallas Stars to win the Cup in 2000. In fact, Ftorek had been fired from the team with eight games left in the regular season.

It was a strange end to the regular season for the Devils, who had racked up a respectable 41–25–8 record with eight games left to go before the playoffs got underway, but the management's decision was final. So Ftorek packed his bags and left the Devils organization, to be replaced by former Montréal Canadiens great Larry Robinson, an assistant coach with the team at the time. The Devils managed only a 4–4 record in their last eight games under Robinson's guidance, and many hockey pundits predicted an early exit from the playoffs that year for the team.

The Devils, however, surprised everyone. Buying into Robinson's defensive scheme, New Jersey choked the life out of its opponents, sweeping the Florida Panthers in four straight, dropping the

Leafs in six games, then the Philadelphia Flyers in a hard-fought seven-game series. The Devils then needed only six games to dispatch the Dallas Stars and win the Stanley Cup.

Ftorek's name was included on the list of team members that was engraved on the Stanley Cup that summer because he had coached the team for pretty much the entire season. No word, though, on whether or not he got to spend 24 hours with the Cup.

Chapter Four

Fanatical Fans

P rofessional hockey could not exist without its fans.

The legions of viewers who tune in every night are superseded in their importance only by the thousands of diehard fanatics who turn out to their teams' home rinks 41 nights out of the NHL season. Those who fork out the cash for tickets, programs and beer are there for one fundamental reason: to cheer on their team.

The mix of people at a hockey game is always eclectic. There are the season-ticket holders who occupy their seats like a home away from home, cheering the team on through its ups and downs. Then there are the less-affluent fans who buy whatever seat they can for any game and become more boisterous in their cheers and criticisms with every drink they consume. There are the legions of young kids, sporting their minor hockey league jerseys, who ignore the game after the first period and instead occupy themselves by kicking a squashed soda can around the concourse. And there are even the odd few who decide that a professional hockey game is the perfect occasion on which to ask the love of their life to marry them.

Although the assembled fans are supposed to play little more than a supporting role in the span of a 60-minute on-ice battle, more than a few have decided to intercede in a game and try to turn the momentum in their team's favour. Fans have assaulted players, referees and league officials to protest some perceived wrong. Some have started strange, obscure traditions that have ballooned into common rituals, while others, emboldened by a few overpriced beers, have simply decided to run around the ice without any clothes on.

Fans come from all walks of life. They are male and female, young and old, rich and working class. They come together for one reason—to do what they can to support their home team and propel them to victory. They just might not always go about it the right way.

This chapter is dedicated to every fan who has ever painted a giant letter on his bare chest, spent the afternoon before a hockey game making a cardboard sign or shed a tear when the home team lost an important game. The boosters described below are most often the exception to the rule when it comes to fan behaviour.

These exceptions, however, prove that hockey is more than just a game. It is a way of life.

Get Ready to Rumble!

With their franchise firmly established in Boston, Massachusetts, the Bruins of the NHL decided it was time to move to a new arena to accommodate the thousands of fans who packed the old Boston Arena for every home game.

On November 20, 1928, the Boston Garden opened its fabled doors to scores of eager fans intent on watching the Bruins battle the hated Montréal Canadiens in the first-ever game in the new arena. The new rink was a vast improvement over the old Boston Arena. The Bruins' old home could barely seat 5000 fans, whereas the brand-new stadium could comfortably seat 13,500 spectators.

Although organizers were expecting a large crowd for the home opener, the throng that flooded the doors of the new arena exceeded their expectations, as well as the building's capacity. By the time the game was ready to start, a full 17,000 people had crammed themselves into the rink, 3500 more than the building was actually capable of holding. While fans inside shuffled and pushed in the standing-room-only crowd for a good view, the mood outside turned ugly. Team officials had finally started turning fans away at the door, and the hundreds still lingering outside the gates quickly became unhappy. Fights broke out as the assembled mob tried to get into the rink any way they could. Members of the Boston Police Department responded and tried to break up the melee, but the fans would not be placated. Fans squared off with police officers, throwing punches and refusing to disperse. Although the police eventually got the upper hand and successfully broke up the crowd, the fans' enthusiasm both outside and in was not enough to bolster the fortunes of the Bruins. The hated Habs went on to shut out the home team 1–0.

Twenty-five years later, crowds would again push and surge in an attempt to watch a Bruins home game, but this time not at the Boston Garden. The roof of a nearby train station had collapsed on February 26, 1952, damaging the arena's ice-making plant in advance of a regular season matchup between the Detroit Red Wings and the Bruins. Rather than cancel the game, officials instead moved both teams and what fans they could accommodate to the old Boston Arena, which had not seen a professional hockey game in 25 years. The rink was filled to capacity as 4000 lucky fans managed to grab a seat for the game, with thousands more turned away at the doors. While there was no violence outside the rink, the outcome was much the same as it had been in 1928. The Red Wings beat the Bruins 4–3.

Hanging Out at a Hockey Game

Whenever there is a sellout crowd at a hockey game, whenever every conceivable space, sitting or standing, is occupied by a body, the broadcaster describing the play-by-play inevitably says the fans are "hanging from the rafters."

This old hockey axiom, however, was actually coined because, at times, hockey fans have literally reached up and grabbed onto the rafters of the rink to improve their view of the game. According to hockey lore, the term was first used to describe fans who would watch the Red Wings play at the old Olympia Stadium in Detroit. The standing-room-only area near the top of the steep-sided arena was not known for having the best view of the game, so spectators intent on getting a better view of the action would reach up and grab the overhead rafters, pulling themselves up and over the crowd. Though it required a little more physical exertion than simply standing where they were supposed to, their perspective of the game was remarkably enhanced by dangling from the ceiling of the building.

This tradition endured until the Olympia was replaced by the Joe Louis Arena for the 1977–78 season.

Making It Big in the Big House

Not every diehard hockey fan can get to the rink for every single home game to cheer on their team in person.

In 1954, the inmates at Michigan's notorious Marquette Prison had no way, short of a jailbreak, to watch their Red Wings play live. On February 2, however, they finally got the chance to see Red Wings greats like Ted Lindsay, Gordie Howe and Terry Sawchuk play live when the team came to the prison for a game.

The idea was the brainchild of prison athletic director Leonard Brumm, who was an acquaintance of Red Wings general manager Jack Adams. The Detroit team travelled to the prison that day and faced off against the Marquette Prison Pirates, a team composed of various murderers, arsonists and bank robbers. All 600 of the prison's inmates were permitted to leave their cells to watch the game.

And how did the prisoners show their gratitude to their hockey heroes afterwards? During the post-game banquet that the team shared with their incarcerated fans, a member of the Pirates presented Red Wings player Ted Lindsay with a "honey bucket," best described as a kind of toilet.

"You guys have made it kind of tough for me to recruit you," Lindsay joked as he accepted the dubious gift.

Gordie Howe Gets Fanned

It's no wonder the Red Wings were asked to play an exhibition game against Michigan's toughest prison crowd. They were one of the toughest teams on the ice.

On January 22, 1955, the Toronto Maple Leafs faced off against Detroit for a regular season tilt at Maple Leaf Gardens in Toronto. While the play was on, a Maple Leafs fan named Irving Tenney decided to insert himself directly into the game, reaching out from the stands and grabbing Gordie Howe's stick. As the two tussled, Howe's linemate, Ted Lindsay, decided to intervene, slashing Tenney in the shoulder with his stick. Rather than give Tenney the chance to back away and surrender, Lindsay decided to punish the Leafs fan for laying a hand on the Red Wings' star player. Lindsay dropped his stick, reached into the crowd and began pummelling the obnoxious fan. Tenney responded, standing up from his seat and throwing punches back at the Red Wings' tough guy. The referee and linesmen were eventually able to get between the two, and Lindsay was escorted from the game.

Lindsay would eventually suffer more than a game misconduct because of his actions. The matter was sent to league president Clarence Campbell for review, and he promptly suspended Lindsay for 10 games, at the time one of the longest suspensions in the history of the league.

Lindsay, however, protested the decision and launched an appeal with the NHL. The suspension was eventually reduced to four games, and Lindsay returned to the ice weeks later.

No one knows what punishment, if any, Tenney received for his actions. He does, however, have a great story to tell his kids and grandkids.

Good Luck is a Dead Octopus

Anyone who has watched a Detroit Red Wings home playoff game has been treated to one of the most bizarre rituals in the entire NHL.

Not a playoff game goes by, it seems, in which an enormous octopus does not come flying from the stands, landing with a sickly, slimy splat on the ice surface.

The tradition of mollusc-hurling and its symbolism actually dates back more than 50 years to a pair of brothers who were the first, in April 1952, to toss an octopus onto the ice at Olympia Stadium. Peter and Jerry Cusimano were the sons of the owner of a Detroit fish and poultry shop. The brothers were also committed Red Wings fans and decided they needed to start some sort of tradition to help the Wings to a Stanley Cup victory that year.

The pair chose the octopus, not because it was quite possibly the grossest animal they could throw onto the ice, but because of the symbolism in the number of its appendages. The eight arms of the octopus stood for the eight playoff victories needed during the 1950s for any team to win the Stanley Cup.

Surprisingly, the tradition caught on, growing in popularity as the Wings of the 1990s began to take the NHL by storm. In June 1995, during the Stanley Cup finals between the New Jersey Devils and Detroit Red Wings, no fewer than 54 octopi cascaded onto the ice throughout the 60 minutes of game three.

While that number might seem high, one particular mollusc of note stands out in Red Wings history. On May 19, 1996, fans Bob Dubinsky and Larry Shotwell somehow smuggled a 50-pound octopus into Joe Louis Arena during the conference finals. It was the largest octopus ever to grace the ice in Detroit, and rink staff decided to honour the gargantuan creature of the sea by placing it on the hood of the rink's Zamboni between periods. Anyone who had missed it before could not ignore the sight of the enormous octopus, spread over the hood of the Zamboni as it made its rounds at intermission.

It's difficult to imagine how one smuggles a 50-pound octopus anywhere.

Montréal Explodes Over Richard Suspension

Maurice "Rocket" Richard was the pride and joy of the entire province of Québec in the 1940s and 1950s. The Montréal Canadiens' scoring sensation was an icon in French Canada, celebrated for his cannonading shot, scoring finesse and fierce, penetrating glare.

The Rocket, however, also had a nasty temper, which landed him in trouble with the league more than once. One particular occasion sparked a public outcry that manifested itself in a night of mob violence, halted only by an impassioned radio plea by the Rocket himself.

On March 13, 1955, the Rocket and the Habs were playing the Boston Bruins in regular season play when Richard was upended by Bruins defenceman Hal Laycoe during one of the Rocket's trademark rushes. When Richard picked himself up off the ice, he immediately sought vengeance on Laycoe, knocking the Boston player to the ice with several slashes. When linesman Cliff Thompson grabbed Richard to pull him away from Laycoe's prone body, Richard vented his fury on Thompson, pummelling the linesman.

Richard was summarily ejected from the game and automatically fined $100. NHL president Clarence Campbell, however, was not about to let the Rocket escape sterner punishment. It was the second time that season Richard had been penalized for assaulting a referee. On March 16, Campbell suspended Richard for the rest of the 1955 season, including the playoffs.

The entire province of Québec was outraged at the decision, but the situation might have cooled off if Campbell had exercised a little more common sense the following day. When the Habs hosted the Detroit Red Wings on March 17, Campbell decided to attend the game with his secretary. The grumbling Canadiens fans took note of the league president's presence at the game and proceeded to hurl verbal insults at Campbell. When the Red Wings leapt ahead to a 4–2 lead, words were replaced by tomatoes, empty cups and programs as the assembled crowd pelted Campbell with whatever they could get their hands on.

No one knows exactly how one fan was able to smuggle a tear-gas grenade into the game. There was a sudden pop at one side of the rink, and the acrid cloud of blinding gas began to permeate the rink. The crowd panicked, climbing over seats and one another to get to the nearest exit. Campbell and his secretary were whisked into a nearby dressing room for their own safety, and the game was stopped.

Outside, the mood of the crowd turned ugly. Loyal Canadiens fans, outraged at how Campbell had treated Richard, as well as at his presence at the game, vented their anger on anything they could find. Hundreds of fans swarmed around the

Montréal Forum, overturning cars, smashing windows and looting shops on Ste-Catherine Street. Fires broke out in the area, and the police were called in to quell the uprising.

As the commotion in the streets continued to escalate throughout the early morning with no sign of abating, Richard decided to take matters into his own hands. The suspended Canadiens star made his way to a local radio station and pleaded over the airwaves for the rioting crowd to stop. When they heard the voice of their hero asking for calm, the fans relented, and the riot quickly dissolved. In the end, 60 people were arrested for causing $100,000 worth of damage to local businesses.

The Red Wings were awarded a default victory by the league because of the fans' actions that night. The two teams would meet again later that year in the Stanley Cup finals, with Detroit emerging victorious after a seven-game championship series.

Mommas, Don't Let Your Babies Grow Up to be Goalies...or Writers!

Many fans have had the opportunity to meet their hockey heroes, but few can say they had the chance to play with them. George Plimpton can make that claim to fame.

During the summer months separating the end of the 1976 season from the beginning of the 1977 campaign, the journalist approached the Boston Bruins with a novel idea. The writer wanted to play in an NHL game and write a story about the experience. After listening to the proposal, the Bruins decided to allow Plimpton to play five minutes in goal during a pre-season game against the Philadelphia Flyers.

Plimpton, however, had never stopped a puck in his life. The writer attended training camp with the rest of the Bruins prospects, trying to learn as much as possible during the short time before he was scheduled to mind the nets against the Flyers. Although he improved enormously as camp progressed, Plimpton still did not feel he was ready when he hopped over the boards to stare down the two-time Stanley Cup champion Flyers.

In the five minutes that Plimpton played, he flopped about on the ice like a fish looking desperately for the nearest body of water. The very first shot on goal, a point shot, was tipped in by Flyers forward Orest Kindrachuk, but it was the only goal the writer-turned-goalie would allow. The Flyers pressed the attack, and the crowd laughed as Plimpton scrambled to stay on his feet, using nearby players to pull himself up after he fell. At one point, when Plimpton lost sight of the puck, he turned his back to the play to see if the puck was actually in the net.

The journalist's five minutes of fame were capped by a penalty shot call against the Bruins. Flyers bruiser Reg Leach swept in on goal, one-on-one against the rookie netminder. Just as Leach wound up to shoot, Plimpton stumbled and fell to the ice. He could not have timed it more perfectly if he had tried, successfully kicking Leach's shot aside.

Plimpton would later say he knew he had truly become a hockey player when he returned to the dressing room afterwards. His teammates had cut the bottoms out of his underwear, the toes out of his socks and chopped his tie in two.

Can We at Least Move Down to the Expensive Seats?

When a true hockey fan has a pair of tickets to his team's next home game burning a hole in his pocket, not even an act of God can keep him from the rink.

On January 22, 1987, the Almighty certainly tried his best to keep the New Jersey faithful away when the New Jersey Devils were scheduled to host the Calgary Flames. The state was pummelled by a vicious snowstorm that dropped nearly 40 centimetres of thick, white powder over the space of a few hours. Roads were closed, and the snow-plows were running overtime, trying to clean up roads and highways choked with snow.

Despite the horrible weather, the game was scheduled to go ahead. In the end, the fans who did make it to the game showed more commit-ment to the Devils than some of the players on the team's roster. Exactly 334 fans braved the weather and took their seats to watch the Flames-Devils matchup. The game was delayed an hour and 46 minutes as Devils players struggled through the weather to the rink. By the time the puck dropped, New Jersey had only 13 of what should have been a full roster of 22 players on the bench, ready to play. What they lacked in numbers, the members of the now-infamous "334 club" made up for in enthusiasm. The sparse crowd cheered the short-staffed Devils to a 7–5 win over the Flames.

Just Don't Lose It

When he was rewriting hockey record books as a high-scoring defenceman, the Bruins Bobby Orr could be described as "out of this world."

In 1996, almost 20 years after Orr was forced into retirement because of a career-ending knee injury, a piece of the hockey star had the chance to actually travel into outer space.

Canadian Robert Thirsk was scheduled to blast off into outer space as a member of the crew of the space shuttle *Columbia* in June 1996. A life-long hockey fan who had revered Orr during his years with the Bruins, Thirsk decided to contact his hero and ask if he could take some possession or memento of Orr's into space with him. The two had never met, but Orr promised Thirsk he would find something to mark the occasion.

A few weeks later, Thirsk received a package in the mail from Orr. Expecting maybe a sweater or a piece of hockey equipment, Thirsk was stunned to find Orr's 1970 Stanley Cup championship ring inside the package.

With the notable exception of the shuttle itself, Orr's championship ring may be the most valuable object to ever breach Earth's atmosphere.

At Least They Weren't Afraid of Rats

Although the players on the 1996 Florida roster wore uniforms depicting a snarling panther on the front of their jerseys, it was the rat that became the team's good luck charm

Prior to the team's 1995–96 home-opener, Panthers forward Scott Mellanby was in the team's dressing room, getting ready for the upcoming game, when he saw a rat scurry across the floor. Grabbing a nearby hockey stick, Mellanby curled the rat in and fired the rodent against the dressing room wall, killing the vermin instantly. When he laced up his skates that night, Mellanby notched two goals in a Panthers victory. After the game, Panthers goaltender John Vanbiesbrouck told the assembled media outside about the incident with the rat, saying that Mellanby had accomplished a rare feat in hockey, a "rat trick."

Florida fans seized on the idea as the Panthers continued to play well for the rest of the season.

By playoff time, the expansion Panthers were ready to make a charge for the Stanley Cup finals, and their fans responded by smuggling rubber and plastic rats into every game. After every single Panthers home goal, the fans would hurl a cloud of fake rats onto the ice. As the Panthers continued to win, the deluge grew increasingly more intense as rink attendants on skates toting large buckets were forced to clean up the hundreds of rodents after every single goal.

The power of the rat, however, could not be denied. The Panthers cruised through the playoffs, straight to the Stanley Cup finals, where they played the Colorado Avalanche. The rink attendants had now been dubbed the "rat patrol" by TV broadcasters, who began timing the speed with which the newly formed anti-rodent force cleaned up the ice after each Panthers goal. In game three of the final series, the phenomenon climbed to new heights as a record 900 rats bounced onto the ice after a Ray Sheppard goal on Avalanche goaltender Patrick Roy.

Sadly, the Panthers' good luck ran out in the finals as the Avalanche swept Florida in four straight games. The NHL responded to the rat craze by pledging any fan actions in the future that delayed the hockey game would result in a minor penalty against the home team.

The Panthers have since been unable to regain the winning form of 1996, the Year of the Rat.

Ron Tugnutt For President

The November 2000 U.S. presidential election was the closest in history and one of the most hotly disputed. Although former Texas governor George W. Bush lost the popular vote to Al Gore, he won the most Electoral College votes after a controversial recount in the state of Florida.

In the state of Ohio, the result was not as close as it had been in Florida, but it was noteworthy for one reason—a Canadian received 12 votes for president.

Ron Tugnutt was a goaltender for the Columbus Blue Jackets in 1996. The former Québec Nordiques puck-stopper had been picked up by the Blue Jackets in the expansion draft and was having an amazing season. In the first month of the season, Tugnutt racked up a 5–1–1 record with a .945 save percentage.

The Columbus Blue Jackets' marketing department decided to use Tugnutt's stellar play to their advantage and began a "Tugnutt for President" campaign, even though the goaltender was of Canadian heritage. That didn't stop some fans from listening to the Blue Jackets' message. When the votes were tallied on election night in Ohio, Ron Tugnutt received a total of 12 votes.

Sadly, the veteran goaltender has yet to visit the White House, either as president or as the netminder of a Stanley Cup–winning team.

Is Nothing Sacred?

Some businessmen will do anything to make a buck.

Brian Price, president of In The Game, a company that produces hockey trading cards, set the teeth of hockey fans and historians on edge in 2000–01 when he acquired the only existing pair of Georges Vezina's goalie pads. It wasn't the fact that Price owned the pads that bothered everyone so much, it was what he was planning to do with them.

Price announced that the pads would be shredded and the pieces affixed to a special limited edition series of hockey cards scheduled for release in 2000–01. A tiny square of the Canadiens goaltending legend's gear would be pasted to the corner of a card honouring Vezina's memory and would make up one of every 2400 cards produced for that year. Other collector cards with similar scraps of memorabilia from goaltenders like Patrick Roy, Pelle Lindbergh and Dominik Hasek were also created for the series.

"I'm as much of a collector, a lover of old hockey as the next guy. This is about sharing the piece with fans around the world," Price argued when the public began to criticize his plans.

"Maybe we can buy enough of [the cards] ourselves to sew the pads back together," Hockey Hall of Fame acquisitions director Phil Pritchard mused in a 2000 news article detailing Price's plans for the priceless hockey artifacts.

A Fan's Flash of Fame

Everyone watching the Calgary Flames home game against the Boston Bruins on October 17, 2002, knew Tim Hurlbut was drunk. Although they hadn't seen him drinking, Hurlbut's actions could only be explained by excessive alcohol consumption.

During a stoppage in play, the inebriated Flames fan decided to display both his team pride, as well as the rest of his body, to the approximately 16,000 fans watching the game. Hurlbut stood up from his seat near the ice, stripped off his clothes, save for a pair of red socks, and hopped the glass separating him from the ice.

The entire crowd watched, half-amused, half-shocked, as the drunken streaker lost his balance coming over the glass and crumpled to the ice. Hurlbut, who would later confess that he was indeed drunk at the time of the incident, fell awkwardly, smacking his head on the ice and knocking himself unconscious. He remained on the ice, completely exposed to the thousands of eyes and dozens of TV and news cameras, for a full six minutes before a team of paramedics carted him away. As they pulled the stretcher towards the waiting ambulance, Hurlbut waved to the crowd that was either applauding his bravery or jeering his stupidity. The image was broadcast on sports highlight reels for weeks afterwards, and many Canadian newspapers ran a photo of Hurlbut's aborted leap on their front pages.

The provincial court judge who heard Hurlbut's case, however, was not as impressed with the Flames fan as the rest of the crowd had been. Reprimanding Hurlbut for the "pathetic spectacle of yourself splayed naked on the ice for six minutes until you were covered," he ordered Hurlbut to pay $2500 to two local charities, as well as perform community service hours.

Chapter Five

Hockey Horror

If you take 50 men, fuel them with desire and competitive spirit, equip them with sticks and razor-sharp skate blades, then place them on a contained, ice-covered battlefield surrounded by thousands of screaming fans, the unfortunate inevitably occurs. Tempers flare, accidents happen and people get hurt. Most incidents of violence are minor in the larger picture of the game: a penalty here, a few stitches there. Injuries heal in time, and the game continues on.

There are some incidents in hockey's great history, however, that have horrified both hockey fans and those who have never taken much more than a passing interest in the sport. In a game where the play hangs on a razor's edge, much can go wrong very quickly. It's easy to think that we would be immune to the short tempers and outrageous outbursts that we witness on television, but until you've put yourself in that same situation and felt the searing stab of a stick across the back of your knee, you will never understand why hockey players do the things they do to one another.

Equipment advances now prevent many injuries that were commonplace in the days of the Original Six teams. Since Jacques Plante first returned to his net in 1959 sporting the now-infamous first face mask, the faces of many goaltenders have been saved from cuts, contusions and broken bones. Helmets for all other players are now mandatory. The last player to play lidless was Craig Mactavish, a former Bruins-Oilers-Flyers-Rangers-Blues forward who now coaches the Edmonton team that gave him a second chance in life and in hockey. The debate now rages around the issue of visors and the size of goaltender equipment. Some claim visors are for sissies, and that goaltender's pads and gloves are partly to blame for the decline in scoring that has become the oft-repeated woe of the sport.

But equipment can only guard against so much. Given the right confluence of events, an injury, whether intentional or not, can still end a player's career.

In 2004, the entire North American continent gasped collectively when Vancouver Canucks power forward Todd Bertuzzi skated up behind Colorado Avalanche forward Steve Moore and brutalized him with a sucker punch from behind. Bertuzzi then fell forward onto Moore, driving

Moore's head and spine into the ice. The image, played over and over again by the sports and news media, inflamed a public that believed Bertuzzi had crossed the line. He was suspended for the duration of the season, on the cusp of Vancouver's playoff run, then charged with assault in BC provincial court. He pleaded guilty to the assault charge and was sentenced to one year's probation and 80 hours of community service. Bertuzzi was reinstated by the NHL on August 8, 2005, and allowed to resume his career. As for Steve Moore, he has since filed a lawsuit against both Bertuzzi and the Canucks organization for damages. His injuries are healing slowly. He has been released by the Avalanche, and it is almost certain that his playing days are over.

Bearing in mind the horror that can stain the beauty of an otherwise unparalleled sport, this chapter recounts some of the league's most terrifying and shocking moments.

Murder on Ice?

Bertuzzi's unprovoked assault on Moore in 2004 did more than place the violence of hockey in the forefront of the public eye, it also reignited the debate on what role, if any, the courts have in dealing with incidents of on-ice violence. Many argued the game should be allowed to police itself, that charging Bertuzzi in a court of law would open up a floodgate of criminal actions and civil litigation for behaviour that had been, until that point, adjudicated by the league. Others felt the incident was proof that hockey teams and players could not be counted on to monitor their own actions—it has been reported in the media that Moore was specifically targeted by members of the Canucks organization for retaliation after he had injured star centre Markus Naslund earlier in the year.

The courts, however, have long extended their reach into the hockey arena when dealing with on-ice violence. On March 8, 1907, teams from Cornwall and Ottawa faced off for a game in the four-team Federal League. As the two teams fought across the length and breadth of the arena for the puck, Cornwall's Owen "Bud" McCourt reached out with his stick and sliced open a five-inch gash on the face of Ottawa's Arthur Throop. As players began to square off for the now too common post-whistle rumble, Ottawa's Charles Masson struck back, cracking his stick over McCourt's head. McCourt fell to the ice, and when the melee died down, he was taken to the dressing room. He returned to the Cornwall team bench several minutes later, then left the game and did not return. Hours later, McCourt died in hospital.

Local officials wasted little time in the wake of McCourt's death. Masson was promptly arrested on one count of murder. Although Cornwall captain Reddy McMillan testified at the trial that

Masson had skated in from 12 metres away while McCourt was fighting with another Ottawa player, other witnesses testified that McCourt may have been struck by another player before Masson got to him.

That was enough for the judge, who believed that Masson "may have acted in self-defence." The charge was downgraded from murder to manslaughter. When the judge returned his verdict, Masson was absolved of the murder in a finding of "not guilty." The judge ruled that the conflicting evidence of witnesses did not sufficiently prove that Masson's attack had been the fatal one, that a previous slash could have also caused McCourt's death. There was enough evidence, it was decided, to show that another Ottawa player most likely struck McCourt first, before Masson's stick made contact with his head.

McCourt would not be the only hockey player to die on the ice, but he was the first.

Shore Silences Leafs "Ace"

He was flamboyant, quick and incredibly tough. Before every home game, Boston Bruins defenceman Eddie Shore emerged from the dressing room onto the ice, clad in a black cape as the Bruins' faithful roared their approval. He was a one-man wrecking crew, a pugilist, a tenacious checker and a gifted scorer.

But for the quick work of doctors in a Boston hospital, Shore might have also become hockey's first killer.

The game between the Toronto Maple Leafs and the Boston Bruins on December 12, 1933, was a rough one. The Leafs, featuring 29-year-old scoring sensation Irving "Ace" Bailey, and the Bruins, boasting Shore as the bulwark of their muscle, were waging battle when both players' lives were changed irrevocably. Shore was working his way up the ice, flying past Maple Leafs defenders and forwards with his characteristic speed and skill, when he was tripped and sent sprawling by a Leafs player, most likely Red Horner. Furious, Shore leapt to his feet and attacked the first player in sight, Ace Bailey. The check was ferocious, as Shore literally dumped Bailey headfirst onto the ice. The resounding crack of skull on ice could be heard across the rink, silencing the soldout Boston Garden crowd. Before Shore could react, Horner swooped in and punched him with all his might. For a brief second, no one moved. There, sprawled on the ice, bleeding from their wounds, were two of the game's greatest talents.

Although Shore quickly recovered from his injuries, Bailey's recovery was much more painstaking and prolonged. In the first hours after the assault, Bailey hovered near death. The prognosis was so poor that a priest was brought in to perform last rites, and Bailey's father hopped the next train to Boston, revolver in hand, ready to kill Shore. Tipped off to Bailey's father's travel plans, Leafs assistant general manager Frank Selke passed on the information to a Boston police officer, who detained the old man when he reached the city.

After two brain surgeries, which were rudimentary by today's standards, Bailey's condition remained tenuous. Boston police quietly began preparing manslaughter charges against Shore, waiting only for Bailey to pass on before apprehending his attacker. Slowly, imperceptibly at first, Bailey began to recover. The swelling of his brain gradually subsided. He would, however, never play hockey again.

In the early days, there was no players' union. Players were paid poorly by today's standards and many worked summer jobs during the off-season to make ends meet. With Bailey's hockey career effectively finished, the NHL decided to help. In what would become the first-ever NHL All-Star Game, the Toronto Maple Leafs played before a soldout crowd against the best players of the rest of the league on February 14, 1934. The proceeds from the game would go to Bailey's family.

A hush fell over the crowd as each player in the game veered towards the boards after his introduction and reached over to shake Bailey's hand. When the name of Eddie Shore was announced, everyone wondered what would happen between the two men. The handshake, however, was friendly, and the crowd erupted in cheers.

Though no longer a player, Bailey became a fixture at Maple Leaf Gardens. He worked in the penalty box area, opening and closing the doors until his death in April 1992.

But Where Did He Keep His Jock Strap?

Although netminders are now swathed in protective gear, the old adage that "goalies are different" endures to this very day. There is something about literally placing your body in the path of a disc of frozen vulcanized rubber that, for many, instantly raises questions about one's sanity.

Modern goalies are not without their quirks, but no goalie can measure up to former Red Wings great Terry Sawchuk. The venerable puck-stopper's athletic skill, his odd personality and his tragic life have made him one of the most memorable characters in the history of the NHL.

Sawchuk is often viewed as one of the greatest goalies in the history of the game. He holds the record for the most career shutouts, and his play in the 1952 Stanley Cup playoffs is often remembered as one of the greatest feats of playoff goaltending of all time. Besides his Stanley Cup wins and his numerous awards and records, Sawchuk holds one NHL record you won't find in the official record books: between 1949 and 1970, Sawchuk racked up 400 stitches, the most in the history of the league. The embattled, bruised and beleaguered netminder waited until 1962 to shield his mug behind a face mask.

His injuries as much as his play have immortalized him in hockey's enduring memory. A rugby injury at a young age, which he delayed having properly treated, resulted in his right arm being two inches shorter than his left. At the end of every NHL season, Sawchuk would undergo surgery to have bone chips removed from his elbow. He proudly kept the bone chips on display in a jar in his home, next to the ether-filled bottle in which his appendix floated.

Sawchuk almost seemed fascinated by the gore of goaltending. On one occasion, after being clipped by a stick and having his eyeball cut open, the netminder was taken to the hospital for stitches. Although the rumour has never been substantiated, the story goes that Sawchuk arranged for medical staff to position mirrors around his head so that he could watch the stitches being put in. Not only that, it is believed the injured eyeball was actually removed from its socket and laid upon his cheek during surgery. Rather than cringe, Sawchuk watched the entire operation, though one would think, given the location of the injury, he would have no choice.

Sawchuk's litany of pain and injury was momentous. He battled mononucleosis as well as a blood infection and suffered a nervous breakdown after his trade to Boston in 1955. His hand was cut open by a skate blade that also sliced through several tendons, a wound that required 79 stitches to close. He played through the 1964 playoffs with pinched nerves in his shoulders, returning diligently to the hospital after every game for treatment. He suffered a punctured lung in a car accident in 1952. In 1966, he had two ruptured vertebrae in his spine repaired and, for the first time in years, was able to sleep through the night without pain.

The goaltender was traded from Detroit to Boston, then to Toronto, Los Angeles, Detroit again and New York before his career ended in 1970. Sawchuk's life was an emotional roller coaster. He battled depression, isolated himself and began drinking to silence the pain in his joints, his muscles and his soul. His wife, from whom he had once separated and then reconciled with in 1958, left him for good 11 years later. Many would later confess they never knew how much Sawchuk enjoyed playing the game. He was one of the best goaltenders in the league, but was tormented by demons he was never able to exorcise.

The circumstances of his death have never been clearly defined. It has been described as both a domestic argument and a play fight, but what is known is that, whether maliciously or playfully, Sawchuk and Rangers roommate Ron Stewart were tussling in a rental cottage on April 29, 1971, when Sawchuck fell. While it is not known if they were horsing around or having a disagreement, it is known that both had been drinking at a nearby pub and had been asked to leave the establishment when they began to argue. During the altercation, Sawchuk fell on Stewart's knee. He was taken to hospital, where his gallbladder was removed, but died one month later at the age of 40 from internal injuries. Police briefly contemplated manslaughter charges against Stewart, but later dropped the matter.

Perhaps in death, Sawchuk's haunted soul finally knows peace.

Bill Masterton's Legacy

In the entire history of the NHL, only one player has died from an on-ice injury, and his legacy has been forever immortalized in one of hockey's most beloved annual awards.

Bill Masterton was a 29-year-old rookie who had been a U.S. college MVP in the 1960s when the Montréal Canadiens sold his rights to the expansion Minnesota North Stars in 1967. Masterton's NHL career, however, would last less than one full season. On January 13, 1968, Masterton's North Stars were playing against the California Golden Seals when the defenceman was checked by two Seals defencemen, Ron Harris and Larry Cahan. In today's NHL, the fall might have left Masterton with a slight headache, but it would not have proved fatal. On this day, however, Masterton fell backwards, his helmetless head bouncing off the ice, then he stopped moving. Ironically, Masterton had worn a helmet during his entire National Collegiate Athletics Association (NCAA) career in the early 1960s.

The blow knocked Masterton unconscious, and though he was immediately transported to hospital, he never recovered. He died two days later with his wife and children at his side.

To honour Masterton's dedication, the NHL created the Bill Masterton Trophy, which is awarded annually to the player who best exemplifies perseverance and dedication to the sport of hockey. Every player in the NHL is now required to wear a helmet so that a tragic death like Masterton's will hopefully never occur again.

A Heart-Stopping Performance

When the horn sounded, there was nothing terribly special about the Flyers' 3–1 win over the Vancouver Canucks on February 9, 1972. It had been a relatively close game, but the win was an important one for a Flyers club that was just beginning to find the momentum that would carry it to two consecutive Stanley Cup championships.

But there was a surprising story to this game that no one, not even goaltender Bruce Gamble, knew about until afterwards. When Gamble complained he wasn't feeling well after the game, he was examined by a doctor. It was later determined that Gamble had actually had a heart attack while playing. More stunning still, the coronary incident had taken place early in the first period, yet Gamble had still finished the game.

The news was enough for the 13-year veteran, who had logged ice time with Toronto, New York and Boston. Gamble retired immediately afterwards and never played another NHL game.

A Very Close Shave

No one who was watching could look away. No one who saw the front page of their newspaper's sports page the next day will ever forget the gruesome picture.

The image of Buffalo Sabres goalie Clint Malarchuk, bent at the waist, trying desperately to stem the flow of blood from his severed jugular vein was one of the most horrifying images ever to come out of the NHL. What compounded the severity of the moment was that, though the injury was purely an accident, it could have likely been avoided by a simple piece of equipment.

On March 22, 1989, the Sabres were playing the St. Louis Blues in regular season action. Blues forward Steve Tuttle broke in on Sabres goaltender Clint Malarchuk, when Sabres defenceman Uwe Krupp grabbed Tuttle to try and stop him. As Tuttle fell backwards to the ice, his skate blade arched upwards and sliced through the skin of Malarchuk's neck. The Sabres goalie reacted instantly, throwing off his face mask and clutching his throat. He fell to his knees as the ice around him reddened with a large pool of blood.

Malarchuk was quickly ushered through the gate directly behind his goal and taken into the dressing room for emergency surgery. The Sabres' trainer later confessed that had Malarchuk been guarding the net at the opposite end of the rink, he likely would have died.

The Sabres goaltender required 300 stitches to close his wound. The injury proved equally ghastly for those who witnessed it firsthand, as two spectators suffered heart attacks and several players on the ice vomited. The entire episode could have been avoided had Malarchuk been wearing a neck protector, now standard issue for most goaltenders.

Most incredibly, Malarchuk returned to the ice only 11 games later to a standing ovation, though he was never the same man. He retired in 1992 and was later diagnosed with obsessive-compulsive disorder. He has since taken up coaching and is now the goaltending coach with the Florida Panthers.

An Amazing Comeback

March 11, 2000, was a date that changed the life of a player viewed as the United States' next best defenceman.

Brian Berard burst into the league with the Toronto Maple Leafs in the 1996–97 season, winning the Calder Trophy as Rookie of the Year for his sterling freshman performance. Although the future looked bright for the young Rhode Island native, no one saw what was coming on March 11, 2000, when the Leafs took the ice against the Ottawa Senators. With five minutes left to play in the second period of what would become a 4–2 Leafs win, Senators forward Marian Hossa stepped into the Leafs' zone and rifled a shot on goal. As he followed through on the shot, however, Hossa's stick caught Berard in the right eyeball, sending the huge defenceman crashing to the ice. Berard was rushed off the ice, a towel pressed against his face and taken to hospital where he underwent emergency surgery. The stick had torn directly through his eyeball, causing extensive vision damage, so much so that the injury was considered career-ending. All hockey players are required by the league to have no worse than 20/400 vision to be able to play.

Incredibly, Berard came back to the sport less than two years after the grisly injury. After five surgeries, he was fitted with a special contact lens that corrected much of the vision in his injured right eye. Berard then signed a multimillion-dollar contract with the New York Rangers. After scoring two goals and 21 assists, Berard was traded to the Boston Bruins.

What truly demonstrates Berard's commitment to the game is his salary—he doesn't draw one. He received a $6.5 million payout from his insurance company for his injury because no one thought he would ever play again. All of Berard's salary since his return has been paid directly to the insurance company to reimburse them.

Chapter Six

Playoff Peculiarities

There are two hockey seasons in the NHL. Only one of them counts.

The regular season counts only insofar as a team succeeds in making the playoffs. Once the team's spot in the post-season is assured, the race for the Stanley Cup takes precedence over a strong finish, a President's Trophy or the fewest goals against. The greatest regular season of all time doesn't mean anything if you're not holding the Holy Grail of hockey over your head in June.

Everything gets better in the playoffs. The beer tastes colder, the games last longer and the wins are by that much narrower a margin. Truly great players lift themselves up past their regular season existence and play even harder, faster and smarter. The best of the best play through triple overtimes and injuries, only to wake up, hop on a plane and do it all over again two days later. Pain heals. Glory lasts forever.

With so much at stake in the post-season, with everyone giving every last fibre of strength in pursuit of the same end, destinies inevitably collide. Not every player who makes the NHL can win the Stanley Cup, but that doesn't stop them all from trying. When two teams bristling with the desire to be the best faceoff in a playoff series, only the gods of hockey can predict the result. Anything can and usually does happen during the four to seven games in between the first faceoff and the final handshake of a series.

The Stanley Cup playoffs have witnessed some of the very best, and very worst, that professional hockey has to offer its fans, all for a trophy donated to an adopted country and sport by a foreigner who shelled out approximately $50 and change for the revered silver bowl. The trophy has since spurred the fantasies of young men across the country. Some have travelled thousands of miles, just for the chance to try and win. Others have rearranged their wedding plans because of an unexpected call to duty.

This chapter will recount some of the greatest, as well as some of the most lamentable, stories that have emerged from the Stanley Cup playoffs. Lord Stanley of Preston, the man for whom the cup is named, never saw a game in which two teams battled for his cup. He was recalled to

England shortly after its purchase. Given some of the stories that follow, it's probably just as well.

The Story of the Dawson City Nuggets

The process by which a team contends for the Stanley Cup has changed little since the NHL took sole possession of the trophy in the 1930s. Prior to the league's exclusive ownership of it, however, any team across Canada or the U.S. could challenge the defending Stanley Cup champion for the chance to win it. Teams from the ECHA, PCHA, WCHL and NHL battled back and forth for years, all vying for the chance to have their names engraved on Lord Stanley's Mug.

In the entire history of the Cup, however, one team's challenge stands out as one of the most dedicated, if futile, attempts of all time. In 1905, a group of men from Dawson City in the Yukon Territory arrived in Ottawa, ready to battle the defending champion Silver Seven for the Cup.

It was a 4000-mile trip to the nation's capital from Canada's most northern reaches, yet that didn't stop the men playing for the Dawson City Nuggets from making the voyage. The team hired Colonel Joe Boyle, a former prospector, to map out the route the team would take. When the Nuggets struck off by dogsled in –20°C weather on December 19, 1904, they did not know whether or not they would win. They only knew they had to try.

The trip, however, was fraught with poor weather and delays. Three of the team's players actually left Dawson City on bicycles, but were forced to walk into Whitehorse when their bikes broke down along the way. The rest of the team travelled by dogsled, completing the 87-mile trip to catch a train to Skagway, Alaska. When the train rolled in, however, the Nuggets learned they had missed their scheduled ferry to Seattle and would have to wait five days for the next boat. They finally did catch their boat, then they boarded a train for the cross-country trip to Ottawa. The team arrived in the nation's capital on January 12, 1905, one day before the Stanley Cup series was scheduled to begin.

Although the Nuggets asked for the game to be bumped back a few days to allow them to recuperate, the Silver Seven refused to delay the start of the two-game, total-goals series. So it was an exhausted Dawson City team that took to the ice on January 13 for the first game. The well-rested Ottawa team skated circles around the Nuggets, winning by a score of 9–2.

If the first game was a blow out, the second was a total massacre. The exhausted Nuggets were simply not as fresh as the Ottawa team against whom they faced off. By the time the final whistle sounded, Ottawa had racked up 22 goals to the Nuggets' three. One Ottawa player, Frank Mcgee, scored 14 times alone in the second game, a phenomenal individual effort made even more so because he had only one eye.

The Nuggets returned home to the Yukon without the Stanley Cup. But the story of their journey and their commitment to winning professional sports' most celebrated trophy were as much a success as a Stanley Cup victory would have been.

A Real Journeyman Hockey Player

Whenever a player goes down on the ice, the rest of the team is responsible for filling whatever hole is left by that player's absence. No player in the history of the NHL, however, has ever stepped up to plug the gaps in a lineup like Frank "King" Clancy did in 1923.

On March 31 of that year, the Ottawa Senators were playing the Edmonton Eskimos of the Western Canada Hockey League (WCHL) in a two-game Stanley Cup final. At the time, Clancy was a second-year player, toting the blue line for the Senators and renowned throughout the league for his tenacity despite his diminutive size. His fighting skill, however, did not measure up to his ferocity. Legend has it Clancy never won a single fight he ever started.

On this night, Clancy's dedication to victory would set a record that has never been equalled. The Senators had already won the first game of the two-game total-goals series 2–1, and Clancy started game two on the bench. It didn't take long, however, for Senators star defenceman George Boucher to go down with an injury. Clancy dutifully hopped off the bench and took over Boucher's position on the blue line. Minutes later, another Senators defenceman, Eddie Gerard, was injured during play. Clancy again came off the Senators bench and assumed Gerard's slot in the lineup.

No sooner had Clancy returned to the bench for a breather than Senators centre Frank Nighbor came off the ice, holding his stomach, winded from the intense play in the game. Clancy didn't need to be asked—he stepped onto the ice and played the next shift at centre ice until Nighbor was well enough to return. Minutes later, Nighbor's linemate, right winger Punch Broadbent, disappeared from the Senators lineup, heading into the dressing room to have a cut over his eye stitched shut. While Broadbent underwent surgery, Clancy assumed his teammate's duties at right wing, even though he was technically a defenceman. When Broadbent returned to the game, Clancy went on to spell Senators left winger and superstar Cy Denneny. Few people other than Clancy realized when he changed up that he had played every single skating position on the ice.

The Senators, however, were not done with their substitute player yet. In the third period, Senators goalie Clint Benedict was assessed a minor penalty by the referee. Although in today's NHL, a player on the ice at the time of a goalie's infraction serves the penalty on the netminder's behalf, during Clancy's era, all goaltenders had to serve their own penalties. The Senators coach nodded to Clancy as Benedict began to skate towards the penalty box, and the tireless 20 year old hopped over the boards and intercepted Benedict. The Senators goalie handed Clancy his gloves and goalie stick and uttered the infamous line: "Here kid, take care of this place until I get back."

Clancy did just that, though he didn't have to work too hard for it. The Senators team surrounded their defenceman-turned-goaltender, blocking shots and checking hard to keep the Edmonton power play away from the net. In the two minutes that Clancy spent as a NHL goalie, he didn't allow a single goal. When Benedict returned to the ice, Clancy returned to the Senators bench, cheering on his team as they skated to a 1–0 victory over the Eskimos to win the Stanley Cup.

After the game, the media milked Clancy's feat for everything it was worth, with one writer stating that Clancy had stopped a breakaway, skated up the ice from his position in goal and taken a shot on the Edmonton net. In the end, Clancy's deed needed no embellishment. It stands as not just a remarkable playoff accomplishment, but a hockey record that will never be broken.

When Will They Invent
Drive-Thru Church?

Sundays and sports have typically gone hand in hand. Whether it be football, baseball, golf or NASCAR racing, men across North America spend much of their Saturday nights trying to develop a believable excuse to stay home from church the next morning.

The Sabbath and hockey, however, have not always been compatible. In 1829, the Supreme Court of Nova Scotia overturned the conviction of a local man charged with playing "hurley," an early form of hockey, on Sunday. The man had been spotted and charged by a local Justice of the Peace on his way to church.

"Every idler who feels disposed to profane the Lord's Day may, now secure from any consequences, turn out with skates on feet, hurley in hand and play the delectable game of break-shins," wrote one outraged citizen to the *Colonial Patriot*.

Religion and hockey would collide again, this time in a much more pressure-packed, violent setting. On March 31, 1951, the Boston Bruins faced off against the Toronto Maple Leafs in game two of the Stanley Cup semifinals. Neither team showed any mercy as the players relentlessly checked, hacked and slashed their way across the ice, tussling in the corners, jockeying for position and possession of the puck. With each trip, each fight and each cut, the whistle blew, stopping the clock just long enough for rink attendants to scurry out onto the ice and scrape up the pools of blood that had begun to coagulate on the surface of the ice.

The unending parade to the penalty box incensed many of the spectators who hollered for the blood of the referee. One onlooker went so far as to leave his luxury seat and descend the stairs to ice level so he could further berate referee Red Storey. That man was W. H. Macbrien, chairman of the Toronto Maple Leafs. At the time he left his seat to exchange words with Storey, Macbrien had been entertaining the Governor General of Canada, Lord Alexander.

Each whistle stopped both the play and the clock, extending the game well past the time it was originally supposed to finish. With the score tied 1–1, neither team was ready to give up, ignoring how banged up and bruised they felt. When the clock ran out on the third period, the score remained tied, and both teams headed into overtime.

It was 11:45 PM Eastern Standard Time when the extra 20-minute frame ended. Both teams returned to their benches for a breather and some strategizing, ready to get back at one another for a second overtime period. As the clock continued to tick towards midnight, however, a small crowd of league officials began to confer with the referee to one side of the ice. Storey talked animatedly with the men for several minutes, then skated over to both teams' benches.

"That's it, boys," he said. "Game's done."

The bewildered teams returned to their dressing rooms, dumbfounded by what had just happened. When the officials finally explained why the game was cancelled, the players collectively shook their heads. The province of Ontario had a law in effect that prohibited playing sports on Sundays. The Leafs-Bruins game was perilously near to the midnight hour, pushing the NHL closer to breaking the law with each minute that ticked down. Rather than pray that one of the teams potted the game winner before the clock struck midnight, the league decided to cancel the game in its entirety.

The match was declared a no-contest—the game was effectively written off and the scores rolled back to zero. The game was replayed the next night with the Leafs blanking the Bruins 3–0.

Hockey's Greatest Mystery

Once the vaunted Leafs defeated the Bruins in 1951, the boys from Toronto faced off against the Montréal Canadiens in the Stanley Cup finals. The Canadiens had dispatched the Detroit Red Wings in six games and were ready to tangle with the Leafs. The two teams traded 3–2 victories in the first two games before the Leafs found their stride. Toronto skated to a 2–1 victory in game three, then edged the Habs 3–2 in game four. Every single game of the series, so far, had been decided in overtime.

The fifth game would also go into overtime, the first and only time in the history of the NHL that every single game of a Stanley Cup final has ever done so. When regulation time came to a close, the Leafs and Canadiens were tied 2–2. At the 2:53 mark of the fourth frame, the Leafs had carried the play into the Canadiens' end when the puck suddenly squeaked out into the slot. Bill "the Kid" Barilko stepped in from his spot on the blue line, wound up and fired, beating goaltender Gerry McNeil to give the Leafs the overtime victory and another Stanley Cup. It was the last goal the Kid would ever score.

In August of that year, the 24-year-old defenceman from Timmins, Ontario, went fishing with family friend Dr. Henry Hudson. On August 24, 1951, the two decided to fly into a remote area of James Bay. With Hudson at the controls, the pair took off, rods stowed, eager to spend a few days relaxing on the water. The two were seen refuelling Hudson's Fairchild 24 in Rupert House, a popular stop for bush pilots flying in and out of Ontario's north.

They were never seen again.

The Ontario government instigated a massive hunt for the pair, but no one could find them.

Leafs manager Conn Smythe used his political connections to Premier George Drew to call out the military, but despite 1354 hours of searching by air in 28 Royal Canadian Air Force planes, the two men were never found.

On May 31, 1962, helicopter pilot Gary Fields spotted the wreckage of a yellow plane while ferrying passenger Ray Paterick from Cochrane to Newpost Creek. When Fields reported what he saw to several local bush pilots, the search for Barilko and Hudson's remains began anew. After a week of frantic searching, the man who had first sparked the search, Gary Fields, again located the twisted wreckage of the Fairchild. Both bodies were found and identified by the medical examiner.

The tale of Barilko's Stanley Cup–winning goal and his subsequent disappearance has since been immortalized by one of Canada's most famous rock bands, the Tragically Hip, in the song "Fifty Mission Cap."

Keep Richard Away From Me!

Maurice "Rocket" Richard was known as much for his physical strength and competitive intensity as his scoring ability. The Rocket's short, often violent temper landed him in the penalty box almost as often as his name was recorded on the score sheet.

In the Stanley Cup finals in 1953, however, Richard's strength and enthusiasm got away from him. The power-packed Canadiens, led by Richard and teammate Elmer Lach, faced off against the Boston Bruins in the Stanley Cup final. The Bruins had upset the first-place Detroit Red Wings in the semifinals, finishing the regular season only six points back of the Canadiens.

The Bruins, however, could muster little in the way of defence to stymie the Canadiens' offensive onslaught. Although they recovered from a 4–2 loss in game one to take game two 4–1, the Habs blanked the Bruins 3–0 in game three, then trounced them 7–3 in game four.

The Bruins were able to keep game five close, taking the Habs into overtime tied 0–0. The extra frame lasted less than two minutes as forward Elmer Lach banged home the Stanley Cup–winning goal. The puck cross the red line; the crowd roared, and Lach raised his arms in celebration.

As his linemates swept around their game-winning goal scorer, Richard was at the front of the pack. He too raised his arms in celebration to embrace his linemate, but something went horribly wrong. The on-ice jubilation came to an abrupt halt as an audible *thunk* swept over the hubbub. One minute Richard was skating in to congratulate his teammate. The next, Lach was being helped off the ice with a broken nose.

As Richard's enemies will attest, a broken nose was a love-tap by the Rocket's standards.

A Bear of a Job

Lach had no idea when he scored the 1953 Stanley Cup–winning goal that he would be exposing himself to injury. In 1959, Habs forward Marcel Bonin duplicated Lach's feat by also scoring the Stanley Cup–winning goal. The celebration went off without a hitch—it was how Bonin spent his summer that proved to be un-bear-able.

The Habs had dominated the 1958–59 regular season, finishing the year atop the league standings, 18 points ahead of the second-place Boston Bruins. The Canadiens easily dispatched the Chicago Blackhawks in the semifinal, while the Leafs eliminated the Bruins. The two Canadian teams faced off on April 9 to do battle for Lord Stanley's Cup.

The Leafs, however, were outclassed by a Canadiens team boasting the offensive might of Maurice Richard, Dickie Moore and Jean Beliveau. With Jacques Plante minding the pipes, the Habs cruised to wins in games one and two. Although the Leafs came out on the winning end of overtime in game three, the Canadiens responded with a 3–2 win in game four. With game five tied 2–2 in the second period, Habs forward Marcel Bonin broke the tie at the 9:55 mark. The Canadiens went on to win the game 5–3 and take home yet another Stanley Cup.

As a playoff hero, Bonin was unremarkable. It was how he spent his off-season that drew the attention of many of his teammates. The Montréal native was an ardent weightlifter who was always flexing his muscles in the locker room. In the summer months, Bonin put those muscles to good use, wrestling bears. That's right, the Stanley Cup–winning goal scorer whose career would eventually succumb to a nagging back injury, who routinely chewed glass in front of his teammates for a laugh, would face off against the great monsters of the forest in the circus ring.

Bonin's bear-wrestling, however, is not the only time an NHL player tested his mettle against one of nature's most powerful animals. In a shameless publicity stunt that speaks volumes about the state of hockey in Canada's small markets, the 1998 Edmonton Oilers decided to sponsor a short game of three-on-three hockey with a troupe of visiting Russian Bears. The Bears' opponents, however, were Russian themselves—million-dollar NHL players Boris Mironov, Mikhail Shtalenkov and Andrei Kovalenko took the ice for the humiliating stunt.

Rumour has it the Oilers trio bear-ly won.

Fog Threatens Cup Final Game

If you were to hear that the May 20, 1975, playoff game between the Buffalo Sabres and the Philadelphia Flyers was almost cancelled because of fog, you'd probably think it was the weather outside that threatened the game's start time.

You'd be totally wrong.

The Flyers and Sabres were facing off for game three of the Stanley Cup finals that year at Buffalo's Memorial Auditorium. The Flyers had jumped out to a 2–0 lead in the series, taking the first two games 4–1 and 2–1. When the series returned to Buffalo for the next two games, the Sabres hoped that having home-ice advantage would help them push back the Broadstreet Bullies' attack.

As the players began to assemble for the evening's game, they became witnesses to a peculiar sight, one that had seldom been seen before in the NHL. The temperature outside the Auditorium swelled to 32°C, and the hot air slowly began to creep into the rink, which was not air conditioned. By game time, the temperature at ice-level matched that of the outdoors, and the heat, combined with moisture on the ice, created an immense bank of fog that blanketed the entire playing surface.

The league considered cancelling the game altogether, but were not about to tell 16,000 ticket holders they would have to go home. Instead, game officials recruited several ice attendants and outfitted them with towels. Every five minutes, during stoppages in play, the attendants would sweep out onto the ice, flailing their towels around in an effort to dissipate the fog. It was ridiculous to watch, but nonetheless effective. The Sabres were able to use the peculiar weather conditions inside the Auditorium to their advantage, beating the Flyers 5–4 in overtime. The Sabres even made a series of it, winning game four to tie the best-of-seven series at 2–2. The Flyers, however, recovered in game five, beating the Sabres in two more straight games to win the Stanley Cup.

The series will always be remembered for the weather phenomenon that almost halted play. When asked after game three what he thought of the decision to carry on with the game, Flyers goaltender Bernie Parent was candid in his assessment:

"I wouldn't take my boat out under these conditions," he said.

Don't Ask What They Did on Their Honeymoon

Any man who scheduled a hockey game on his wedding day would probably find himself standing at the altar alone. Yet that's exactly the predicament rookie Steve Rooney found himself in during the spring of 1985. The Providence

College student had proposed to his girlfriend the previous year, and the two picked April 13, 1985, as the day of their blessed union.

The Montréal Canadiens, however, had other plans for the young man. The Habs were in the thick of a playoff battle against their long-despised enemies, the Boston Bruins. With the injury bug feasting on the Canadiens roster, the Habs were forced to call up some of their prospects to plug the gaps for game three of the series. One of those players was Steve Rooney.

Unfortunately, the day of Rooney's first NHL game happened to coincide with that of his wedding. The Canadiens and Bruins, however, did their best to make the day one of the happiest in Rooney's memory. Rooney and his wife were wed on the morning of April 13, 1985. Rooney was then escorted to the Boston Garden by members of the Boston Police Department, where he arrived in time to suit up for the playoff game. Rooney decided to create his own kind of hat trick for the day: the rookie had already married the love of his life and skated in the NHL, wearing the jersey of the most famous team in sports history. He decided to cap the day off in fine form, scoring his first-ever NHL goal in a 4–2 Habs win over the Bruins.

The rest of the playoffs were a blur for Rooney, who alternated Canadiens' playoff games with the demands of being a husband and writing final exams for his degree in business administration.

The Habs' playoff run was aborted by the Québec Nordiques in the next round, but Rooney had made an impression—he had earned himself a full-time spot on the Canadiens roster for the following year.

Get the Puck Out of My Way!

The 1987 Philadelphia Flyers were a team of destiny, and no one was going to deny them a berth in the Stanley Cup finals, especially not the Montréal Canadiens.

The Flyers and Canadiens met up in the Wales Conference finals in May 1987. The winner would go on to meet the Edmonton Oilers in the Stanley Cup finals.

The Flyers, propped up by the stellar play of rookie goaltender Ron Hextall, were eager to do anything they could to disrupt the play of the Montréal Canadiens, the defending Stanley Cup champions. During the pre-game warmup for game six, the Flyers decided to take action before the opening faceoff.

Hockey players are prone to repeating bizarre rituals if they believe that performing the action will, in some way, benefit their play. During the 1986 post-season, Montréal forwards Shayne Corson and Claude Lemieux developed a ritual in which both players would wait for the opposing team to leave the ice after the pre-game warmup. When the rink was clear, either Corson or Lemieux would sail one last shot on the opposing team's empty goal.

On May 14, 1987, the Flyers decided to mess with destiny. As the pre-game warmup began to wind down, Flyers backup goaltender Glenn "Chico" Resch and brawler Ed Hospodar inserted themselves between the Canadiens' end and the Flyers' goal, preventing Lemieux and Corson from completing their ritual. The four began to exchange words on the ice. When word of the confrontation reached both the Flyers' and Canadiens' dressing rooms, players came pouring back out onto the ice, facing off in ones and twos. The brawl took several minutes to break up, both teams were sent back to their dressing rooms.

Before the game even started, the NHL had issued $24,000 in fines to the players involved in the melee. The Flyers didn't even bat an eyelash at the total and went on to defeat the Canadiens in the Wales Conference finals. The team of destiny ran out of gas against the Oilers, however, dropping the Stanley Cup finals four games to three.

Who Turned Out the Lights?

Only two playoff games in the history of the NHL have been cancelled in their entirety. The first, in 1951 between the Boston Bruins and Toronto Maple Leafs, was suspended because of a rule prohibiting anyone from playing sports on Sunday.

The second, 37 years later, again involved the Bruins.

The Boston Bruins had finally dislodged a 43-year-old monkey from their collective backs in 1988. The Beantown boys had finally beaten the Montréal Canadiens in a playoff series for the first time since 1945, dispatching the Habs in five games. The Bruins faced off against the defending champion Edmonton Oilers in a seven-game series that would decide the year's Cup champion.

Although the Oilers ultimately defeated the Bruins four games to none to capture their fourth Stanley Cup in five years, the mighty Oil actually had to play five games to win the series. Edmonton had beat the Bruins in the first three games by a combined score of 12–6 and, on May 24, were looking forward to winning their second straight Stanley Cup on the ice at the Boston Garden.

The Bruins kept it close, skating with the Oilers and tying the game at 3–3 heading into the third period. At the 16:37 mark, without warning, the lights in the Boston Garden inexplicably went out. The entire arena was plunged into darkness as the power failed throughout the building. It was as if the building knew what was coming and could not bear to watch the Bruins lose the Cup on home ice.

The emergency lights eventually clicked on, providing enough light for fans to leave the building. There was no way, however, the game was going to be completed. Rather than halt the game and resume it at a later date with the score tied 3–3 with only a few minutes left in the third period, the league ordered both teams to replay the game in its entirety. Although the game had been played in Boston, the replacement game was played in Edmonton, where a packed Northlands Coliseum watched Wayne Gretzky and the Oilers double the Bruins 6–3 to win yet another Stanley Cup.

Chapter Seven

Stanley Cup Sensations

I t is the most celebrated of all trophies, the most revered of all prizes in sports. Young boys across Canada, the United States and now the world dream about it at night, closing their eyes and imagining what its fine etchings and dented frame would feel like beneath their fingertips. Lord Stanley of Preston paid approximately $48 and change for it, and it is now insured by the NHL for $75,000.

It is the Stanley Cup—hockey's most hallowed trophy.

And how do hockey's elite celebrate their hockey supremacy when they are blessed enough to win the Holy Grail?

They treat it like a garbage can.

Perhaps the Cup's history of abuse is what has enshrined it in the collective mind of the Canadian people—that even a trophy considered sacred by some has spent its share of time sitting in the Rideau Canal or at the bottom of Mario Lemieux's swimming pool. Each strange tale of the Cup's travels, each player who has decided to try and immortalize himself forever by scratching his initials on the inside of the Cup has only added to the trophy's mystique. Although the NHL has since hired escorts or "Cup cops" that now travel with the Mug 24/7, part of the fun of winning the Stanley Cup is being able to do something with it that no one else has ever done. Each beer that is quaffed, each fried chicken wing picked from the bowl, only adds to the Cup's magic, to its accessibility to the common man who will never have a chance to do something like that...unless Mark Messier happens to bring it to a favourite strip club for a drink.

It seems fitting then, in this book's final chapter, to honour some of the funny, strange and terrible things that have been done in, to and with the Stanley Cup.

How It All Got Started

In the late winter of 1905, the Ottawa Silver Seven had just finished off the Dawson City Nuggets in a two-game, total-goals Stanley Cup final. The Nuggets had travelled 4000 miles by dogsled, foot, bicycle, ferry and train to challenge the Silver Seven for the Cup, only to lose by a combined score of 31–5. After finishing off the Nuggets, the players on the Silver Seven decided to celebrate their victory at a nearby restaurant and, in a custom that has since become synonymous with winning the Cup, had a little too much to drink during dinner.

On the walk home after their celebrations, one of the players grabbed hold of the Stanley Cup, took two steps, swung his leg back and punted the silver bowl into the nearby Rideau Canal. The players laughed drunkenly and tottered off, more intent on finding their own beds than the trophy they had just kicked like a football.

Fortunately, when the players awoke the next morning and remembered what they had done, the Cup was still where they had left it. The Canal was frozen, and the trophy lay among the dead rushes protruding from the ice and snow.

The Healthiest Thing to Ever Occupy the Cup

The following year, the Silver Seven relinquished their Stanley Cup supremacy to the Montréal Wanderers, and the Wanderers players decided to commemorate the occasion with a team photo. They took the Cup to a photographer's studio in Montréal and mugged for the camera with the Mug. When the players left the studio, however, they forgot to take one very important item with them—the Stanley Cup.

After months of tearing apart their homes and closets, searching for the priceless trophy, one of the players finally thought to check with the photographer to see if he knew the Cup's current whereabouts. The Mug was exactly where the team had left it, though the photographer had made one small change in the Cup's use. He had taken the trophy, filled it with earth and was now using the bowl to grow a beautiful bouquet of flowers.

Sadly, the photographer had to return the Cup to the Wanderers players. There's been no word on what happened to the flowers.

"I Thought You had the Cup!"

There was a commercial on television several years ago for a Canadian brand of beer that showed a young man and his friends stumbling across the Stanley Cup during a night of drunken revelry, then taking the trophy on an extended road trip. The commercial is most likely based on the fact that if any average Canadian found the Stanley Cup just sitting somewhere, the person would probably take it for a drink as well. It is as much a Canadian reflex as being polite or pointing out that we burned down the White House during the War of 1812.

But on a cold night in Montréal in 1924, no one walking down the street noticed the small silver bowl sitting by itself on the street corner. In fact, the men who had left it there did not even notice it was missing until much later that evening.

In 1924, the Montréal Canadiens finally won what would become their first of 24 Stanley Cup championships when they defeated the Calgary Tigers of the WCHL 8–1 in a two-game, total-goals Stanley Cup final. After returning to Montréal from the final game in Ottawa, the Canadiens players headed to coach Leo Dandurand's home for a party to celebrate their victory. Several players travelling in the same car to the festivities were, however, delayed when one of the car's tires went flat. The players all dutifully piled out of the car and set to work changing the ruined tire. The Stanley Cup was placed on the sidewalk to free up as many of the players' hands as possible for the task. Within minutes, the tire was fixed, and the players crammed themselves back into the car and drove off.

And the Stanley Cup sat on the side of the road, watching the car disappear.

It was not until the team reached Dandurand's house and someone, no doubt, asked the players, "Where's the Cup?" did they realized that they no longer had it in their possession. The players all jumped back into the car and roared back into Montréal. Fortunately, the Stanley Cup was still sitting at the side of the road, patiently waiting for its newest owners to return.

Don't Ask What They Drank Their Champagne Out Of

The 1947 Stanley Cup finals played out exactly the way a championship should.

The Montréal Canadiens, the NHL's first-place team, faced off against the Toronto Maple Leafs, the league's second-best club, for bragging rights in the Stanley Cup finals. The series lived up to the hype in the first two games as Canada's top two teams traded shutout victories. The Canadiens, however, stumbled in the stretch, and the Leafs took a 3–2 lead in the series, with the final game to be played in Maple Leaf Gardens on April 19.

Leafs general manager Conn Smythe, however, was not about to watch his team blow the Stanley Cup final because they were overconfident. He berated the team after their 3–1 loss in game five and then issued an order he would never regret— Conn Smythe ordered the Stanley Cup left behind in Montréal.

The aim of his directive was simple, if a little heavy-handed. Smythe felt the Leafs were so assured of victory, they were coasting into the end of the series. By leaving the Cup behind in Montréal, the Leafs had to work that much harder to realize their goal of winning Lord Stanley's Mug.

The strategy, though strange, paid off. The Leafs' Ted Kennedy potted the game-winning goal against the Canadiens in the third period to defeat Montréal 2–1. Although the Leafs celebrated their victory with the home crowd, their festivities were somewhat muted—the Cup was still in Montréal. In the 88 years of the NHL's existence, 1947 is the only year in which a team won the trophy, but was not presented with it immediately following their victory.

Only a Habs' Fan...

Criminal activity of any sort can never be condoned, but Ken Kilander may very well be the Montréal Canadiens' greatest fan of all time.

The Montréal resident was seated in the stands at Chicago Stadium during game six of the 1961 semifinal series between the Canadiens and the Blackhawks, trying not to pull out his hair. The Habs were losing to the Hawks—again—and were now on the brink of being eliminated from the Stanley Cup playoffs altogether. Chicago goaltender Glenn Hall was coolly turning away Montréal shots by the dozen, working on his second consecutive shutout, when Kilander finally snapped.

The lifelong Canadiens fan left his seat and worked his way down into the lobby of Chicago Stadium before the game ended. He stood there in the lobby, in front of the Stanley Cup, wallowing in sorrow, despairing at the idea of any team other than the Canadiens winning the coveted trophy. Rather than accept his team's fate, Kilander decided to act. He reached out, grabbed the Cup from its unlocked case and dashed towards the exit.

Policemen patrolling the Stadium saw Kilander running away with the Stanley Cup and quickly apprehended him. When the Canadian fan was brought before a local court the next morning to explain his actions, Kilander issued one of the most famous statements ever made by a hockey fan: "Your honour, I was simply taking the Stanley Cup back to Montréal where it belongs."

The judge sternly noted that, while the Cup no longer belonged in Montréal, Kilander certainly did, and ordered him to return home.

Don't You Know Where That Cup Has Been?

Leonard "Red" Kelly was a busy man in 1964.

The Toronto Maple Leafs defenceman-turned-centre not only played in the NHL for one of hockey's oldest franchises, he was also a member of Parliament for the Liberal Party, representing the people of York West in Ottawa.

The dual demands of professional hockey and governance were often difficult to meet, no more so than in the spring of 1964. The Leafs had just defeated the Detroit Red Wings in a hard-fought, seven-game series, shutting out the Wings 4–0 in the final game. While the rest of the team celebrated their championship, however, Kelly could not. The MP for York West was needed in Ottawa for a vote the next day and left the rink shortly after the game.

Harold Ballard was prone to instances of compassion from time to time, and when he saw Kelly defer his Cup celebrations to represent the Canadian people in the House of Commons, he decided to reward Kelly for his devotion. Ballard hired a photographer to go over to Kelly's house and take pictures of Red and his family with the Stanley Cup. Kelly was overjoyed, even going so far as to prop his infant son up in the bowl of the Cup for a photo.

When Kelly took his son out of the bowl, however, it was not empty.

"He did the whole load in the Cup. He did everything," Kelly revealed in a later interview. "That's why our family always laughs when we see players drinking champagne from the Cup."

Kelly's kid is not the only person in the history of the League to use the Cup as such a dubious receptacle. The New York Rangers allegedly took turns urinating in it following their victory in 1940.

No Spell-Checker for Silversmiths

For those fans who think the Stanley Cup is a perfect, unblemished trophy, they need only look in a few select places.

Yes, the Cup has been dented, watered, soiled, scratched and taken apart and then put back together again, but there are several blemishes on its gleaming surface that take a slightly more trained eye to detect.

Some teams no one has ever heard of have apparently won the Cup. In 1963, the Toronto Maple "Leaes" bested everyone else in the league for the Cup honours. Ditto for the 1971 "Bqstqn Bruins," as well as the New York "Illanders" in 1983. NHL records show the Toronto Maple Leafs, Boston Bruins and New York Islanders actually won the Stanley Cup in those same years.

The team names, however, are not the only names to be misspelled on Lord Stanley's Mug. Legendary Canadiens goaltender Jacques Plante, the man who introduced the face mask to the NHL and backstopped the Habs to five consecutive Stanley Cup championships, has only had his name correctly engraved twice on its exterior. Although the 1955 and 1957 rosters correctly identify "Jacques Plante" as the Canadiens goaltender, Plante was apparently replaced in 1956 by "J. Plante," in 1958 by "Jac Plante" and again in 1959 by "Jacq Plante."

Plante does not stand as the only player to have his name misspelled by a clumsy engraver. Leafs forward Ted Kennedy, who scored the Stanley Cup–winning goal in 1947, was rewarded for his efforts by being forever immortalized in hockey history as "Ted Kennedyy" on the Leafs' roster. Canadiens two-way specialist Bob Gainey, who played for the Habs through the 1970s and 1980s, was also the victim of a careless silversmith, recorded on the Canadiens' roster as "Bob Gainy."

Peter Puck Almost Pulls a Fast One

Only one person, however, has ever had his name removed from the Stanley Cup. It was not a player or a coach, not a general manager, scout or water boy.

If you look closely at the names of the 1984 Edmonton Oilers team engraved on the side of the cup, you'll notice a series of 16 "X"s on the list of names. The name underneath the string of "X"s is that of a man who never played for the Oilers, or any other NHL team for that matter. The name is Basil Pocklington, the father of former Oilers' owner Peter Pocklington.

Pocklington always protested his innocence on the issue, claiming the engraver had mixed up the team roster with a list of individuals who were to receive replica miniature Stanley Cups. Knowing

Pocklington, however, it is not beyond the realm of possibility that the former meat-packing mogul tried to pull a fast one on the league. The NHL was not impressed and ordered the name removed from the Oilers' 1984 band.

By today's standards, however, Pocklington's attempt to honour his father, whether intentional or otherwise, pales in comparison to the lists that are engraved on the side of the Cup. Everyone from the coach to the administrative staff to the teams' scouts to accountants and trainers are just as likely to have their name etched on Lord Stanley's mug as a player who actually played for it.

No more blatantly was this demonstrated than in 1997 when Detroit Red Wings owner and pizza-chain magnate Mike Ilitch had not only his own name, but the names of nine family members engraved on the side of the Cup.

It isn't known whether one of those relatives is named "Little Caesars."

Oh, the Places You'll Go

The Cup has come a long way since it was first purchased and donated to Canadian hockey by Lord Stanley of Preston. It has endured countless beatings, dentings, droppings and submersions. It has been left overnight on someone's front lawn and used as a toilet bowl.

The following are some of the more interesting things people have done with Lord Stanley's Mug or places they have taken the Cup in recent history.

Mark Messier has always loved women, and women seem to find him even more attractive when he's holding the Stanley Cup. In 1990, when the Gretzky-less Oilers proved their mettle by besting the Boston Bruins in the Stanley Cup final, the "Moose," his teammates and the Cup made an impromptu stop at the Forum Inn, a former strip club just east of Northlands Coliseum in Edmonton, to celebrate. Messier repeated the feat in 1994 when he captained the New York Rangers to victory over the Vancouver Canucks, visiting several nightspots with his teammates, including—that's right— another strip club.

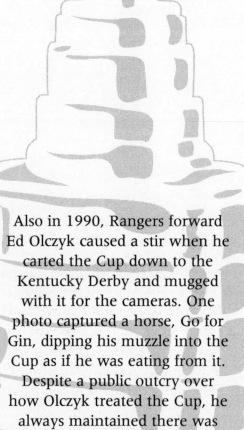

Also in 1990, Rangers forward
Ed Olczyk caused a stir when he
carted the Cup down to the
Kentucky Derby and mugged
with it for the cameras. One
photo captured a horse, Go for
Gin, dipping his muzzle into the
Cup as if he was eating from it.
Despite a public outcry over
how Olczyk treated the Cup, he
always maintained there was
nothing in it when he held it
up to Gin's mouth.

While Go for Gin may not
have eaten out of the Cup,
Hombre the German shepherd
has. The pooch feasted on a
bowlful of Ken-L-Ration from
the trophy, courtesy of owner
and New York Islanders
forward Clark Gillies.

Players themselves are not above eating from the Cup. In fact, it is as much a tradition as drinking from it. The list of foods that have been slurped from the sloped sides of the bowl include: Cheerios, Fruit Loops, Cap'n Crunch, fries and gravy, poutine (fries and gravy with cheese on top), raw oysters and lobster bisque.

The Stanley Cup, thank
goodness, is rustproof. This has
been proven on several
occasions when players felt it
necessary to somehow bathe
with the Cup. The Mug has sunk
to the bottom of two pools: that
of Penguins star and owner
Mario Lemieux and that of
Colorado Avalanche goaltender
Patrick Roy.

Not everyone can say they've showered with Detroit Red Wings captain Steve Yzerman, but the Stanley Cup can. The Red Wings longest-serving active player apparently toted the trophy into the tub during his 24-hour stint with the Mug.

Still others have used the
Cup for more spiritual
purposes. In 1996,
Avalanche defenceman
Sylvain Lefebvre had his
baby daughter baptized in
hockey's Holy Grail.

Several players have also taken
the Stanley Cup overseas,
where the Mug enjoys as
much popularity in other
countries as it does at home.
Devils forward Scott Gomez
took the Cup home to
Anchorage, Alaska, zooming
through the city on a dogsled.

The Cup has also been to both Europe and Asia. Russian forwards Vyacheslav Fetisov, Vyacheslav Kozlov and Igor Larionov, once-feared forwards who played for the former Soviet Union, took the Cup into Red Square in Moscow. Peter Forsberg has toted the Cup back to Onskoldvik, Sweden, while former Dallas Stars backup goalie Roman Turek took the Cup all the way to České Budějovice in the Czech Republic.

NOTES ON SOURCES

Allen, Kevin. *Why is the Stanley Cup in Mario Lemieux's Swimming Pool?* Toronto: Penguin Books Canada, 2000.

Anstey, Robert. *The Stanley Cup: A Historical Look at the Most Coveted Prize in Sports.* Sardis, BC: West Coast Paradise Publishing, 2003.

Davidson, John. *Hockey for Dummies.* Foster City, CA: IDG Books Worldwide, 2000.

ESPN (n.d.). www.espngo.com. Retrieved May 15–June 21, 2005.

Everything You Wanted To Know About Sports (n.d.). www.hickoksports.com. Retrieved April 15–June 21, 2005.

Fischler, Stan. *Cracked Ice: An Insider's Look at the NHL.* Chicago: Masters Press, 1999.

Fischler, Stan. *Offside: Hockey From the Inside.* Toronto: Methuen, 1985.

Hockey (n.d.). www.canada.com/sports/hockey/. Retrieved April 20–June 21, 2005.

The Internet Hockey Database (n.d.). www.hockeydb.com. Retrieved April 13–June 21, 2005.

Klein, Jeff Z. and Karl-Eric Reif. *The Hockey Compendium: NHL Facts, Stats and Stories.* Toronto: M & S, 2001.

Maguire, Liam. *What's the Score?* New York City: Random House, 2001.

McFarlane, Brian. *The Best of It Happened In Hockey.* Toronto: Stoddart Publishing, 1997.

The National Hockey League (n.d.). www.nhl.com. Retrieved April 14–June 21, 2005.

The Official Home of the National Hockey League Players' Association (n.d.). www.nhlpa.com. Retrieved May 1– June 21, 2005.

Podnieks, Andrew. *Players: The Ultimate A–Z Guide of Everyone Who Has Ever Played in the NHL.* Toronto: Doubleday Canada, 2003.

Poulton, J. Alexander. *Canadian Hockey Record Breakers.* Montréal: Éditions de la Montagne Verte, 2004.

Shea, Kevin. *Barilko: Without a Trace.* Bolton, ON: Fenn Publishing, 2004.

Weber, Dan. *The Best Book of Hockey Facts and Stats.* Buffalo: Firefly Books, 2004.

Weekes, Don. *Red Hot Hockey Trivia.* Toronto: Douglas & McIntyre Publishing, 2003.

Weekes, Don and Kerry Banks. *The Best and Worst of Hockey Firsts.* Toronto: Douglas & McIntyre Publishing, 2003.

Weekes, Don and Kerry Banks. *Hockey's Most Unusual Records.* Toronto: Douglas & McIntyre Publishing, 2002.

ABOUT THE AUTHOR

Peter Boer has been a consummate hockey fan since his parents first bribed him with a chocolate bar to skate from the red line to the blue line at the age of four. It took him three years to score his first goal, but he never looked back. Since realizing actual talent was a necessary requirement for an NHL career, Peter has immersed himself in the game in other ways. He has refereed and minded the score clock for beer-league hockey, coached women's hockey and been a goal judge, penalty box staff, security guard, ticket taker and blood cleaner for the CIS University of Alberta Golden Bears and Concordia University Stingers.

When he's not spending his Saturday nights bemoaning the current state of the NHL, Peter covers sports, as well as politics and news for the *St. Albert Gazette*. He is the author of three other books, including *Bush Pilots: Canada's Wilderness Daredevils* and *Canadian Spies and Spies in Canada*.